BEIRUT,

for my dearest irene

so.. this is my story

post the sanctuary of our

lovely art room ☺ dearest

irene... you are a true

friend. a strong and

beautiful woman. life

is tough, but also beautiful.

you are an inspiration.

stay strong.
stay beautiful.

xxx

peace

ok, i know i used
strong + beautiful
like 3 times,
but... uh...
i *really* mean it.

:)

ZENA EL KHALIL

Beirut, I Love You

SAQI

London San Francisco Beirut

First published by Saqi, 2009

CLOTH EDITION: 978-0-86356-455-0
PAPERBACK EDITION: 978-0-86356-415-4

A full CIP record for this book is available from the British Library.
A full CIP record for this book is available from the Library of Congress.

Manufactured in Lebanon

SAQI

26 Westbourne Grove, London W2 5RH
825 Page Street, Suite 203, Berkeley, California 94710
Tabet Building, Mneimneh Street, Hamra, Beirut

www.saqibooks.com

Dedicated to my sister, Lana

Thank you for letting me steal some of your precious memories.

Thank you for always finding the strength to keep me on my feet.

Thank you for being a free spirit and my backbone.

Thank you for loving Beirut a thousand times more than me.

It is raining. Outside on the windowsill tiny puddles of rain are gathering and then falling off, and then gathering up, and falling off again like mass suicides. The sound of the waterdrops banging against the window is overwhelmingly loud; as loud as the rumors.

Maya Ghannoum

1

There is a thin line between reality and dream.

When I was born, my father gave my mother a necklace. It was in the shape of an anchor. Many years later, I lost this necklace. I had taken it off my neck during a basketball game, and someone stole it off the bench. I was furious with myself that the object symbolizing my birth was lost in such a pathetic way. This was a sign of things to come. Things that I loved, I would continue to lose.

Sometimes I wonder if that necklace actually existed. Sometimes I wonder if I am even real. I look down at my hands and my feet, they confirm that a body exists, but I can never see my face. I stare into mirrors only to be met by a pair of ordinary brown eyes. If I stare long enough, the eyes become those of another being. On the other side of the mirror, I step out of myself. This game scares me and I turn away after only a few seconds. It is terrifying to come face to face with yourself – to see what you really are. That you could be real. That your responsibilities are real. That your life is truly out there.

Interacting.

Existing.

I don't remember my birth, I don't remember how this all began, but I do remember how I died. I remember how I died before returning to this world as the person I am now. I went from darkness to darkness, then to light. But now it is dark again.

Amreeka, you exist now. But nothing lasts forever.

Maya, you will always be in my heart. In my blood.

Beirut, you are just like me. Walking that thin line. Your heart is big, but it is that heart that will bring you down. Beirut, I am your parasite, competing for love.

Eventually one of us will have to concede.

While you revel with your warmongers who have blood on their hands, I will steal your wine and poetry.

The poet always wins.

The poet always wins.

I remember the moment I decided to become an artist. It was not easy. My family was all about numbers and profits. The arts, poetry and literature were not taken seriously. But that fateful trip to Rome in the mid-80s, the one planned as a shopping extravaganza, altered my fate. I remember, fluorescent earrings and hefty shoulder pads were in fashion. Walking along Via Condotti and Via Veneto, my mother sensed that I had a longing in my spirit that boutique shopping could not satisfy. So she took me to the Vatican. To Saint Peter's Cathedral. And then I saw Michelangelo's Pieta. That did it for me.

I was convinced.

I have a picture of myself standing in front of the statue (in those days it wasn't hidden behind a glass façade) holding a brown-and-black-striped Fendi handbag. Looking into the Virgin's eyes, I knew I was destined for other things better than the piece of leather hanging off my left shoulder. I looked up at Mom holding my hand, making sure I didn't wander off, and thought that we had finally made a genuine connection. Her dark hair was frizzy from the heat, and

I could see little beads of sweat accumulating on the fringe of her forehead – on regular days, Mom would never get caught like this. She is like Sophia Loren in both looks and spirit: the "*queen of all that is good and fair*". I love that woman.

Both of them.

I looked at the Madonna and thanked her for bringing Mom down to earth for at least a few minutes because it was then and only then that I realized that I had to become an artist.

2

My story starts with the oldest lifetime that I can remember. I was born in 1901 and my name was Hussein.

My past lives always feature a grand love story. Hussein's great love was New York City. Even now I can recall how badly he wanted to go there. Somehow this desire carried through to my two subsequent lifetimes. Some things never go away.

New York has always brought me big surprises, but not the kind dreams are built upon. They are not covered with glitter and stardust. They are illusions. These surprises are always about death and the challenge of rebirth. About suffocation, fear, stale bread, fungus-ridden bedspreads, obscurity, loss of purpose.

New York always represents a certain type of freedom. One that does not seem to exist in the Middle East. New York is always about people being people: drinking coffee, walking their dogs, painting, reading, hanging out, studying, working, eating, meeting, growing, running in the park, laughing, loving, living. What I've grown to learn – the hard way – is that New York can also be a monster.

During my present life, begun in the second millennium, the super empire of the world has done its best to create television shows to convince me that my life in Beirut is not adequate. That I am missing out on things. That Beirut is just not good enough. Television New York is glamour and success. It is being an individual carving out your path in life. It is a great gang of reliable friends. It is the joy of being middle class and independent. Finding and following your dreams. Navigating through Corporate Amreeka.

Making money.

Making it big.

Anything short of a "non-fat-grande-café-mocha-latté-hold-the-sugar" was just not good enough.

But New York City is also an illusion.

New York does not welcome everyone. It is selective about who it takes in. It will claim your soul in return for a high rent you cannot afford. New York will put you into a category. It will make you fat, short, black or white.

It will make you Arab.

Two lives before this one, when I was Hussein, I was traveling to New York to meet my parents. I was not yet an artist. It would be eighty-two years before I'd meet Maya. And ninety-four before I'd experience my first war.

I was a young boy from an obscure village in the Lebanese mountain range. And like most oriental tales would state: my parents were betrothed to each other at birth. This part is true; however, it is the story of how I was conceived that is unusual. According to the story, one day my mother was out in the fields picking whatever fruit was in season. Every telling of this story recalled a different fruit; cherries, apples, raspberries, pumpkins, olives, once even eggplants. Regardless of the produce in question, the story goes that her dress somehow caught on fire; some say it was matches, others say the reflection of the sun on her ceramic skin. Miraculously, she was unhurt. She jumped out of her dress and found herself standing stark naked in the middle of the orange, lemon, cucumber, broccoli, artichoke, clementine, (*insert fruit or vegetable of choice here*) field. Her toes tingled upon contact with the soft earth. A shiver shot through her, turning her nipples hard. My father caught sight of her and was immediately aroused. Then, I was supposedly conceived under the fig, plum, or almond tree, depending on the teller of the story.

How these two star-crossed lovers ended up in New York City many years later is a mystery. Why they left without me I do not know. But somehow, sometime later, they got lucky and found some wealth in the New World and felt it was time to bring me over. I was eleven years old.

I traveled with a friend of the family who agreed to help me make the voyage. His name was John Abilmona. His real name wasn't John. It was one of those things Arab men did before they joined the New World; take on a Western nickname so that they could successfully climb the ladder. Anything less than John, Mike, or Steve wouldn't get you through Amreeka. Anything sounding remotely oriental will ensure that you stay where Amreeka thinks you belong. John's real name was Nassif. How Nassif translated into John is unclear. However, there are some names that translate quite well; Mustapha becomes Steve, Mohammed – Mike, Fadi – Freddy, Mazen – Mark, Firas – Frank, Mounzir – Joe, Dawood – David, and Ossama – Owen.

Nassif Kassim Abilmona was a proud and good-looking young man. He took pride in his name as a youth. He came from a long line of successful merchants. However successful his family was, Nassif (John) could only afford a third-class ticket for the *Titanic*. Because I was a minor, I rode on his ticket – number 2699. I remember the ticket master growling at us as we purchased it, "No Arabs, no dogs".

Maybe that is why Nassif rode the *Titantic* as John. I just kept my mouth shut.

A day before, I left the warmth and serenity of farmland life and journeyed down to sophisticated Beirut – a port city and prostitute at the same time. I had no idea it could be so beautiful. There were fat men in red felt fez hats and plump women adorned in turquoise make-up with eyes lined and dripping in kohl.

I would go on now to describe the food, aromas and spices that wafted through the air, but I promised someone that in this book, this Arab woman writer would make no mention of food, spices, aromas or being veiled. I'm talking about me now, the author in her present life, and not the little boy who was conceived under the jasmine/cactus/walnut tree. This particular Arab woman, who often talks about herself in third person, experiences her city in more realistic ways. To hell with romance and nostalgia. To hell with grandma's secret recipes. This Arab woman hates cooking. This Arab woman scorns Arab women who express themselves through food. I don't have time to sit all day and pick lentils. I don't have the need to discuss feminine hygiene with the village women. I can go for weeks without showering. I can drink a bottle of wine all by myself. I don't have time to roast eggplants and crush garlic. I can't be bothered to pick a fight with Israelis when they claim that hummus and falafel are their inventions.

But to get back to the story of Hussein ... I was a boy when I rode the *Titanic*. They say that you usually reincarnate into the same sex, but this rule does not pertain to me. History tells me that my name was Hussein. History also tells me that boys named Hussein have a history of premature deaths.

I met up with Nassif at the port harbor and we embarked on a journey that would change my life. What happened to the *Titanic* is well known, so I will spare the details of how the heart must go on. What I will tell, however, is how I drowned. Not many people can describe that.

I am afraid of the ocean to this day. I am afraid of open water. I am afraid of the dark and I blame it all on the *Titanic*, because, yes, I still remember drowning. It is true what they say about drowning. It is quiet. It is excruciatingly personal. The loudest part of the night was when we hit the ice. There was an ear-splitting crack that resonated throughout the ship – louder than any bunker buster or sonic boom. After we hit, it was fairly silent from that point on. True, everyone was screaming, but I couldn't hear them. My eyes and ears were fixed on the dark black sea. I began to let go of bits and pieces of me. I knew I was going to die and found peace with it quickly. I thought about my parents briefly, huddled in bed together, maybe not even sleeping because of their excitement to be reunited with me. I thought about Nassif, who was trying to get me on a lifeboat. I thought about what was going on in his body. I saw his blood flowing from one vein to another. I saw his dinner being churned into shit. I wondered if he was going to survive all this. While we climbed out of steerage, I rode on Nassif's shoulders. I was flying above the crowd, everywhere below me, reflection of tears shimmered against the walls. The water had already begun to pour in. It was a turquoise blue, not the blackness I would later encounter.

Riding above the crowd was surreal. They no longer looked like humans. It was just flesh pressed against flesh.

A giant orgy.

A festival of human excrement.

When man recalls his tales of bravery in history books, he often speaks of the sword that pierced the heart, the shield that protected the truth, and the courage that pushed through the fear. What they fail to mention is the reality of how the human body copes with pressure. About how the intestines turn flaccid. About the loss of control. The involuntary vomiting, The weakening of the stomach. The taste of bile. The taste of acid. The feeling of hopelessness and despair. The fear that prevents action. The coldness of the palms. The throbbing in the head. The tears, the shit and even more shit. I floated on his shoulders peering at those around me; I accepted I was done for. I wasn't angry. I just knew.

If truth be told, it wasn't until I started drowning that I became incredibly scared. The fear was not of death, but rather of being in such a dark and expansive space. The sea was so big. So endless. And as I fell deeper, it grew darker; the silence deafening.

I think about it today, I realize I decided when it was time to die. I remember thinking to myself that I was ready to accept death simply because I could not stand being in this silence. It was the silence that killed me, not the sea. It was truly a lonely death.

What I remember most was the color of the water.

It was purple.

Nassif (John) is a *Titanic* survivor. He is one of the 705 people to survive. He did not drown like the other 1523. His corpse does not lie beside mine at 4000 meters below the sea. It took twenty-six Christmases, New Years and Ramadans before Nassif could forgive himself enough to tell his tale.

He had placed me into a lifeboat. He was planning to join me on that same boat once he got to the water, where he was sure he would be able to bypass the "women and children only" rule. He slid down the rope that hung next to my lifeboat, number "15", as they lowered it into the water. I never lost sight of his eyes. He timed our descent, determined to reach the water at the same time I did.

At precisely 2.43 AM lifeboat "15" became entangled in her own ropes, jamming her to a halt. Lifeboat "4", directly above her, and unaware of the commotion below came crashing down on top of it. None of the passengers in my lifeboat survived. Nassif watched in horror as it splintered into a million pieces. I caught his eyes a second before I went under. It was the last time we ever saw each other.

It took Nassif twenty-six years to talk about his pain. Finally, in 1938, he agreed to an interview with a local newspaper in Roxboro, North Carolina. The article is still available today, although it is not entirely true. Nassif spoke broken English and lived with the burden, the shame, of being a survivor. Men were not supposed to outlive the sinking of the *Titanic*, especially not steerage-class men.

Indeed, the article is a polished version of Nassif. For example, it states that Nassif was already married to a woman, Najmeh, who bore him five daughters: Jamal, Dalal, Souad, Wedad and Samia. The truth, however, was that Nassif was not yet married to Najmeh when he crossed the Atlantic on the *Carpathia* after being rescued from the *Titanic*. At the time, he was married to his first wife, Salha, who miraculously gave birth to his son Mohammad (later known as Mike) on the very same night the *Titanic* went down. Believing he had not survived, Salha left Nassif's family and eventually remarried.

Nassif met Najmeh several years later on a trip back to Lebanon. They married and Najmeh gave birth to Wedad who eventually gave birth to May who eventually gave birth to me, Zena, the author, in this present life.

As Hussein, I lay at the bottom of the sea for almost five-and-a-half years. I wandered in the darkness all by myself, searching for the glitz and glam they called New York. I could not find it. I walked for years to no avail. My legs grew thin and my heart, weary. I grew blisters the size of continents. I walked and walked until I forgot why

I was walking. This New World would not have me, alive or dead. I broke down. I was tired and lonely. And lost. A hazy memory came back to me: "No Arabs, no dogs".

It was not meant to be.

I closed my eyes and thought of my parents. I am sorry I could not be with you. I am sorry I let you down. I did not want to seem like a failure, but for how long could I continue with this game? How long did I need to walk in order to be convinced that I was not welcome?

Enough was enough, I decided.

I picked myself up and started walking east. I crossed the Atlantic and squeezed through the Straits of Gibraltar. I walked past Malta and her great cliffs. The language began to sound familiar. I passed between the islands of Greece and it was there that I overheard them speaking of an invasion into the crumbling Ottoman Empire. I picked up my pace and ran by the Anatolian coast until I could take it no more. Somewhere between Syria and Beirut, I decided I had reached home. It was November 23, 1917.

I surfaced to life in the form of a baby girl with endearing blue-green eyes. I had spent so much time underwater, that I brought something back with me. Sea births were dangerous at the time, and there was little chance of my survival, but my new parents were determined to keep me this time. And so they named me *Amal*, meaning "hope". The rest of the world came to know me as Asmahan.

3

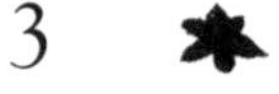

It was not easy being a Druze woman when I lived as Asmahan and it is not easy being a Druze woman now.

Coming from a long line of proud and conservative histories, we have always been praised for our patience and moral behavior and valued for our self-control. We've stood by our men, our fierce and noble warriors who protected our Levantine mountains from alien invaders. We were humble intellectuals who studied the writings of Socrates, Jesus, and Mohammad. We were pious and serene, believing that our lives on Earth were but a fraction of a moment in time, believing that one day, after all our reincarnation cycles, we would finally be reunited with our holy maker. We lived in villages and farms. Our hands strong and brown from years of toil under the sun.

There was a time when we enjoyed equal status in society with men. We debated Plato's theories under grapevine pergolas during Indian summers. We taught our daughters how to cook and sew, as well as how to read and write. We took long strolls in wheat fields on cool spring nights. We read poetry around the *oujeq* during the freezing winter, feeding it wood to roast our potatoes and garlic.

Change happens, but sometimes it takes centuries for us to notice.

When the Ottomans came, we played along with them. Until one day, one of us betrayed our community. He took it upon himself to rewrite our codes of conduct, to reform our society to better fit the Ottoman lifestyle. Some say he did it in order to protect our community, to make us conform so that we could survive. To conserve our religious and social identity.

But at what price? Because, due to his actions, our women lost their equality and turned into domesticated rabbits. We no longer questioned, we obeyed.

According to our reformer, in order to be perceived as a righteous woman, we had to be soft-spoken and mostly silent; bashful, untainted and above obscenity. We were instructed to never confront our husbands with any ailments. We were told to always be poised and self-possessed, yielding when reprimanded and obedient when ordered. We were to let him manage our affairs and never stare at him, always be modest with him and exhale when looking at him, be compliant with his opinions and love him with ultimate sincerity, favor him over our parents, forgive him when he wrongs us and receive his anger with compassion. Above all, we must not rejoice when he stumbles and always approve of what he says and what he does. We were coerced to detest extravagance and be content with abstinence.

Our reformer imposed these rules on us and, presently, we still live under the shadows of his decree. Our women today have done very little to try and attain their previous status within the community. It is a shame the way religion suppresses people. And it has become so difficult to separate religion from government these days. In Lebanon they have become so fused together it is almost impossible for our citizens to challenge the systems they live under. It has become almost impossible for women to live the lives they deserve.

As Asmahan, living almost one hundred years ago, I tossed these imposed reforms out the window. I wanted to have nothing to do with them. For me, singing was my god.

My husband.

My home.

My existence.

And anyone who offered venues for me to sing in: my prophet. And Cairo, she was my New York.

Cairo played push and pull with me. I wanted her, but she was always just out of reach. Every time I thought I was getting somewhere, every time I had a new opportunity to perform and sing, something would happen to push me back down. The rumors, the lies, the scandals. The pressure from my conservative family to keep me off the stage. To keep me off the silver screen. It was the '30s and I was connecting with my sisters across the Atlantic. The world was changing and moving. And at such high speeds. I could see it all unraveling in front of me. The cars, the trains – machinery at its most glorious state. Televisions in every home. This was the new god. The power of the moving image had the world mesmerized. If they could do it there, why couldn't I do it in Cairo?

We were just as modern as New York City. In fact, we were older and wiser. We were the story spinners. Everything started and ended here.

But tradition is heavy and burdensome.

I began to drink. A lot. I could out-drink most people at a party. I was always the last to leave. I often passed out. Or, more accurately, blacked out. I began to lie. To trick my husband so I could run away for a night and sing. I drank to gain strength. I drank to forget. I drank to live a level of existence that I could not find without drink. It helped me find my voice.

And keep it.

I sang in bars. I sang at parties. I sang for private audiences. I sang to movie directors, hoping to win their favor. I sang for my mother and brother. I sang for all the men in my life and for all the women too. For my family in Syria who were considered royalty. Royalty, but with no money. I sang to get away from tradition. Years and years of heavy tradition. Tradition that is lifeless. Sticky. Burdensome.

All I wanted was to feel alive. To sing. To dance. To drink. Life was changing so quickly and I wanted to change with every second of it. To hell with village life ... I wanted to perform in front of a deserving audience. I wanted to sing to the Egyptian farmers who truly understood the simple life. Who always smiled and sang back. I wanted to be on television. In movies.

But my oppressive family always did their best to keep my wings clipped. To keep me obedient and untainted.

The Middle East has not changed much in the last 200 years. We are still fighting the same wars, but we've given them new names. Life as we know it began with us. We are the center of the universe and everything has to spring from here first. We have the burden of giving birth, while the rest of the world enjoys fixing our birth defects. They have learned how to take the fetus, inject it with the latest technology, and watch it grow into a megalopolis.

As Asmahan, I often felt torn between the two worlds of the East and the West. My heart, my heart was rooted to my land. But I sang to build bridges. While the French and the British and Germans fought their macho wars on our land, I sang about love. To my family, the brave warriors who guarded the Syrian and Lebanese mountains with their lives, I asked them to make peace with our European guests. The world was changing and we had to adapt. I truly believed that life could exist without turbulence.

Like Hussein on the *Titanic*, I died a premature death. Unlike Hussein, I always envisioned my death. I knew it would come too soon. I knew it would be an accident. I knew it would be on a road. I even knew which road. On many occasions I'd heard my funeral song. I often sang it to myself. The only thing that caught me by surprise was the timing. It was when I least expected it.

But that is always the way with death.

4

Eighty-nine-and-a-half years after the sinking of the *Titanic* and fifty-seven years after my car accident, I found myself standing in front of the Twin Towers when the first one fell. I was on 6th Avenue and had a clear view. Close enough to see, but far enough to be safe. To be exact, I was on the left side of Ray's Pizza, in front of a truck.

It was crowded and we knew that we shouldn't be there, but there is something grossly disgusting about man's interest in experiencing disaster. I say experiencing because it seems like disaster can only happen through an experience. It is never black and white. It is usually hard to define. And for each person, it happens in a unique way. Some participate through the reaction of their emotions, or in some cases retraction. Some run to join the fight, others retreat. Some look when they know they shouldn't. Some are simply voyeurs. Some cannot comprehend the situation and seek to make associations with something they already know.

I grew up watching Amreekan action movies. I grew up with Schwarzenegger and Rambo. With Bruce Willis and Chuck Norris. With Charles Bronson, Lee Marvin, Jean-Claude Van Damme, Jackie Chan and Eric Roberts. With MacGyver and Mr. T. With *Magnum P.I.* and *Top Gun*. *Hunter*. *Air Wolf*. *Mission Impossible*. *Die Hard*.

Miami Vice. They have taught me that in times of trouble, one may hear the following expressions:

> Shit, holy shit, shithead, shit for brains, fuck, fuck me, fucking hell, what the fuck, fuck you, fuck you asshole, cocksucker, oh my god, Jesus help us, holy-mother-of-god, bastard, bitch, son-of-a-bitch and yippie-kay-yay motherfucker.

I heard all of them and more on September 11, 2001. It was an action movie. Looking around me, I saw people faced with their worst nightmare. They were scared and confused. Some had their eyes closed. Others open. Some sat on the curb crying in disbelief. Others ran through the streets with their hands flailing in the air. There were children too. Not too many because most were at school, but there were the few who woke up late that morning and were still on their way. People pointed. People hugged each other. Some had their hands covering their mouths. Some whispered. Some threw up. I realized how similar we all were. All of us around the world. How we all feel fear and grieve and mourn. How, when faced with a crisis, we often lose everything we've spent our lives working to become. A man was no longer an executive in a business suit. He was Kurt, who was dyslexic, the son of Amy and Joe. Brother of Danny and Nicole. She was Christine, daughter of Joyce and Brian, and not an art historian. We all held hands, holding on to strangers who suddenly seemed like our closest relatives. No, we weren't that different after all.

I think the people of New York City didn't know how to react at first, because nothing like this had ever happened to them before. Panic took over, like it does with people all over the world when they are faced with a spectacular crisis. And when panic took over, judgment was thrown out the window and that is when people started pointing fingers.

Fear, betrayal, confusion, guilt, pain, loss, anger – these are universal emotions after all.

SUBJECT: From mom
To: zena
Wed, 9/12/01 11:32AM 2KB

Hayati zanzoona, Hayat albi Lannossi

I can't tell you the horror we are living and the fear of the consequences.

Every one is glued to the TV, every one is giving his or her point of view, people are shocked, every one is concerned and worried about their direct relatives or their close people. Lines are jammed. I could not get through to you. I received all your emails and Lana's. Zena and Lana, please understand that your movement should be restricted at this stage and please Lana, calm down at this stage. O'f!!!! I do not know what I am saying I know that you are not little children to take any risks but I am worried and I have no idea what will be the reaction of this tragedy. Food for example. I know that people panic in a case like that. Anyway please keep me updated. I am staying home today. I am glued to the screen of the computer and the screen of the TV. I love you. Take care and please try reaching aunt Nabila and the people that would like to hear from you.

Bye hayat Albi and take care. Do not

```
end up eating nothing but Pizzas. 1 LOVE
YOU
```

```
SUBJECT: where are you
To: zena
Wed, 9/12/01   7:52 PM    1KB
```

```
Mamesito Zanzooni,
  Where are you? I have not heard from
you! Please e-mail . I can't get through
the telephone. I have not as well heard
from Lana. I hope e-mail lines are not as
well out !!!!!!. Love you, Mom
```

New York was not the same. After the two buildings fell, I was seen only as an Arab. At school they came up to me asking if I could explain why it all happened. On the streets, people walked far away from me in fear that I may jinx them with my black-and-white-checkered *kuffiyeh*. It seemed that the more people hated Arabs, the more I wanted to be one. The more questions people asked me, the more stories I told them.

I told them about how the Amreekans blew up my mother's house in 1983. My mother, who had nothing to do with all this. My mother who had, only ten years before the explosion of her home, won the regional beauty pageant. My mother who once dreamed of making love to Clint Eastwood. Her brother, who dressed like John Travolta, his room plastered with Hollywood pinups. His white pants bursting with his sexuality. His masculinity that could never behave behind his zipper. His hair, a black bulky heap. His hairspray, endless. His gels, infinite.

House gone.

Brother and sister, the whole family, homeless.

House blown up by the USS *New Jersey* in 1983.

The USS *New Jersey* who had once fought in Vietnam.

Who once shelled targets on Guam and Okinawa. Who raided the North Korean coast. "Big J", after being modernized to carry missiles, found her way over to our Lebanese shores and blew apart my mother's house. Oh "Big J", you fifteen battle star ship, why did you crush my mother's memories? "Big J", "Big J", you creamed my mother's house. Her clothes and toys. Her favorite mascara. "Big J": now a museum, once a proud and mighty killer. "Big J", did you even know my mom, or were you so filled with hate you fired blindly? Like an asinine man, enraged, but restricted by his limp dick, you wanted to take out your anger. Banging your head furiously against a concrete wall until it bled. Imagining that every pretend ejaculation was the birth of a new era. Eyes red and bulging, drunk in a furious rage. Missiles hard; penetrating. Saliva; bountiful and smelly. Skin; stiff, coarse, crackling, open sores, pus, blood, excrement. "Big J", you aging bastard, you shat on my mother's house. You took away all of her belongings. All of her recollections. The red Tupperware in the kitchen. And even the brand new linen.

I told them that when I watched the first building fall, my only thought was if I'd ever see my lover again. I did not register the people on fire. I wasn't afraid of dying. I did not register the 200 people jumping out of the windows. I did not see the falling man. I did not register the firefighters trapped under the buildings. I thought about my lover in Lebanon. My pretend-lover who did not care to love me back. My lover whom it took six long days to finally be bothered to email me to see if I was OK. My lover who once claimed to be a sniper, was only, in reality, full of shit.

After the first building fell, I painted what was going on in my head. I painted my lover, who was not gracious enough to call and ask about me. Who could not even be bothered to write. I painted the panic in my heart. I painted the fear of being Arab.

I didn't have any canvas and was too afraid to walk to the art supply store on Canal Street, a stone's throw away from the Twin Towers. Did the store even exist anymore? I found an old roll of paper in someone else's studio. I cut away two meters, left a pink thank you post-it note, and tacked the paper up to the wall in my studio. The paint, watered down, almost tore through the paper. I would paint a layer and then wait for it to dry. Then go at it again. It took hours to finish. By the time I was done, it was well past midnight. I thought I was alone in the building, but then Tim walked into my studio. Drunk on beer.

"How can you paint now?" His voice choked.

"I need to express myself." I lowered my brush to the ground.

"What about all the people who died?" He leaned against the wall and slowly started to sink down until he was squatting with his back to the wall.

"People die every day, this event is nothing new. Buildings fall in Lebanon everyday. If we stopped painting whenever there was a crisis, we would no longer have art. Lebanese painted during the civil war. I am painting now."

I tried to tell him in the most compassionate way that I could, but it came out all wrong. So cold and indifferent and not what I was trying to get across. I tried to tell him that I too was afraid. That this was all new to me too. That death and destruction is always a unique experience. It is always a surprise. There is always a deluge of emotions that follows. That I had been locked up at home for the past week because I was too afraid to be on the streets. That we were eight Arabs living in my apartment for five days because we were afraid of being mobbed. We were afraid of being alone. That I wanted to get drunk too, because it was too much to take in. That I was afraid to drink because I didn't want to lose control. That it was too difficult to speak, and he was asking questions that I was not sure how to answer. Everyone it seemed was asking me questions. Questions because "I was one of them". Because I was Arab.

Tim was angry and confused. Sitting down in the corner of my studio he started peeling away the label on his bottle. His eyes were red – from crying, from drinking, I don't know. His hair, the color of East European pilsner, was ruffled and hung over his tender blue eyes. He looked like he was nine years old. He looked afraid. He couldn't understand how I could be painting. And really, neither could I. But it seemed my only escape. I was an Arab in New York City. I wanted to hide, but people were asking me too many questions. I wanted to hold Tim in my arms and kiss his forehead, like a Madonna, and let him know that things would pass and that he was going to be all right.

Like a mother cradling her child who has received a racial slur for the first time, I wanted to tell him that there are bad people out there and that we have to learn how to be strong. That people die. That buildings are blown up all the time, all around the world. That in Palestine, people are killed every day. In Palestine, children die for no reason. In Palestine, children are killed by bulldozers demolishing their homes.

Is there that much difference between a plane and a bulldozer?

But Tim, like most of my classmates, was suspicious of my affection. As their hearts filled with fear and suspicion, my heart grew bigger. I wanted to love. I wanted to take everyone, sit them down and gently burst the bubble they had been living in. I wanted to be the mother who sits her daughter down and informs her about how one day boys may try to kiss her and do other naughty things. I wanted to tell my classmates about South Lebanon, Palestine, about Sri Lanka, Burma, about South America, and Africa. I wanted to ask them if they remembered Bosnia and Iraq. I wanted to ask them if they remembered their very own Native Americans. I wanted to tell them that people die every day and that what happened in New York City on September 11, 2001 was no different.

But I guess it was. Somehow. Somehow. After that day, the whole world changed.

But how could I know that then?

Being an Arab in New York in the year 2001 was the shock of the icy water all over again. It was being classified as a third-class citizen one more time; trapped in steerage. And then, like the time before, I started to drown.

But this time I was a little more prepared. I appropriated a *kuffiyeh* and wore it loud and proud. I let my hair down, my long, dark, curly, nappy, nifty Arabic hair. My hair that was my voice that spoke on my behalf. My Arabic hair that drifted down to my hips. I wore kohl on my eyes. I drew henna patterns all over my hands with a black permanent marker. I became oriental. I belly danced to rap music. I seduced men by talking of fruits, spices and cooking. I spoke of our olive trees and about how we don't use pesticides in Lebanon. How everything is fresh and good. About climaxing during prayer.

The more New York repelled me, the more I wanted to be me. The more Amreeka wanted to crush my species, the more I wanted to breed. The more "*Bush*" in the way, the more I hacked out a clearing. I was not going to go down like this. I too worked hard to get to where I was. I was not going to let everything slip away because of stereotypes. New York, why could you not remember the best thing about you? Why could you not remember that you belonged to everyone?

When the stereotype was placed on me, I decided it was time to explore it, in order to expose it. I painted men with guns. I painted women with guns. I painted children with guns. The whole world was going to hell and I was leading the way. I was carving the path for revolutionaries and free spirits. I was waving the red flag. I was liberty leading the real people. The whole world was on fire and I was burning brightest. I painted in purple and pink and gold. I painted all day and all night. I drank more than I painted. I was a woman vexed. I was a woman determined to live. I would not let New York win this time. I would not let her steal my life. It was not my time to go. I knew it when I watched the first building fall. I knew it when people stopped talking to me. I knew it was not going to end like this. I knew that when I died this time, it would not be *here*. It would not be anywhere close to *here*.

New York, I believed, was more than this. There was a good side to this city and I would not let myself be overcome by one really bad disaster.

There were cherry blossoms and divine conversations. There were parks and children and people who had purpose. There were creative people, active people, and inspiring people. People who were proud. Who worked so hard to get to where they were. People who put faith in their lives and the system they chose to live in. People who had conviction in the other people around them. People who gave up everything just to be part of this great city. People who believed. People like Iyad.

Iyad represented everything that was good about New York. At the tender age of sixteen, he came to Amreeka from Lebanon, to pursue the glorious dream of independence and self worth. Or maybe, just like the many before him, without realizing it, he was simply running away to something better.

Iyad owned a chess shop in the middle of Greenwich Village and was the proud owner of four shirts, two pairs of jeans, a couple pairs of socks, some underwear, and a pair of black sneakers. He took pride in the fact that he didn't need material objects in order to survive in the big city. It was his heart that would take care of everything. Iyad thrived on love and giving love.

His day began at around 4.30 PM when he would wake up, wash his face, brush his teeth and then run to the post office before it closed. After his daily mail check, he continued with his day, slowly trying to catch up with the world around him. Iyad had been living in New York for over sixteen years, without ever having returned home. When I think about it today, I understand the daily mail stops. I wonder if anything ever came from home. Many years later, I tried to send him a gift from Lebanon, but he never got it. I believe that somewhere in Amreeka, there is an underground chamber where they dump all the mail coming from the Middle East, or anything with Arabic writing on it. Maybe they even have incinerators to burn away any proof of existence. I wonder if Iyad ever received anything from home after 9-11. Probably not.

The first time I met Iyad was in a secondhand bookstore just off Union Square. I was homesick, browsing through the Middle East section. It was strange to see Arabic books placed right next to Israeli ones. I guess that was the way of New York. Everyone had to find a way to live together, and somehow they usually did.

Just to my right, a man of average height and weight was sitting on the floor surrounded by stacks of books he had taken off the shelves. I couldn't tell how old he was. Maybe my age, maybe a little older. I could tell right away he was Arab as he opened books from right to left and scanned them backwards. It was bizarre. He was slightly balding and wearing a black polo shirt and a pair of worn-out jeans. I stood staring for a few seconds and just as I realized this was rude and started to turn away, he looked up and our eyes locked. It was embarrassing, but instead of glancing past him, minding my own business, I looked into his chocolate eyes and asked him in Arabic, in a very casual tone, as if we had been friends forever, how he was doing.

"*Keefak?*"

"Good," he replied. "Great, actually. I have been looking for a book about Ziad Rahbani for years in this store and I still haven't found anything."

"So, why are you feeling so 'great' then?" I asked.

"Because I just met you."

Yes, Iyad was a poet-flirt of New York City. I could not take my eyes off his; now realizing he was definitely older. There was too much sadness in them for someone in his twenties. It would have been excessively unfair, but also not so uncommon. No one had ever been so direct with me before. It was a wonderful mix of Arab masculinity and Amreekan assertiveness. I liked it.

"I feel like I'm in one of those long Amreekan movies," I said. "This conversation could never have happened back home. This kind of moment can only happen in New York, right?"

"You may be right to some extent that this is definitely a New York moment, because, well, under the circumstances we are presently in New York City, and time is passing between, through, under, and around us," he said, "but as for this long Amreekan movie you just mentioned, our meeting has only just begun, and if you already think I am boring and long-winded, I can tell you right now that this is the beginning of a beautiful friendship. You only just met me, but already I can hear you lecturing me as if we have been married for fifty years. Yes, yes, I think we're off to a great start. Have a seat by my side, my young Lebanese student, and let us start our adventure together."

"How did you know I was Lebanese and a student?" I asked.

"Because of your accent and the way you said hello. It was too casual to belong anywhere else in the Middle East. Also, you have homesick written all over your face. Come on, let's get out of here and let me buy you some dinner."

"Um ... no, it's OK. I have to get back to work." Was he hitting on me? I didn't feel comfortable. I'm not one to pick up strange men in bookstores.

"It was nice meeting you, good luck finding the book." With that, I turned around and marched out. I was feeling flustered and my face betrayed my embarrassment. I had a big smile and my heart thumped 600 miles-per-hour. It felt so good.

"Wait up," he called after me. "Where are you going?"

"I have to study. It was nice to meet you." I practically ran out the bookstore, laughing and shaking my head.

Yes, it felt good.

And suddenly, I found myself wrapping my arms around New York wanting to give everyone a big hug. I had made a connection to the city and did not feel alone anymore. It is amazing how it changes your perspective on everything. Suddenly everyone around me was smiling and happy. Where did all the angry people go, I couldn't see them anymore. I ran all the way home. Home. I was calling it home now. It felt good.

When the buildings fell, I ran away to paint. When the buildings fell, Iyad ran towards them. All he wanted to do was help. He helped wipe the white dust off of people as they ran towards him. He helped firemen carry their equipment as they ran towards the buildings. And when the buildings fell, he helped search for their bodies. For five weeks, he spent every night at Ground Zero, helping.

A few years before the buildings fell, I ran into Iyad again. Actually, he ran into me. I was standing in front of the glass windows of the Museum of Contemporary Art in Soho. I was staring in to see if I could see any work, without having to actually fork up the $8.50 to go inside. As I looked into the windows, I noticed a reflection staring back that wasn't my own. This reflection was slightly balding and wearing a black polo shirt. My heart leapt. But I didn't turn around. I guess I was afraid to come face to face with my destiny.

"I know you can see me. Don't be afraid. I am not stalking you. I am not hitting on you. I am just very homesick as well. You are the closest thing I have seen to Lebanon in over a decade and a half."

"I don't even know your name," I said, my back still turned.

"Iyad," his reflection said.

"Iyad, that is a nice name, but it's too close to home. I was just starting to get used to this city. Just starting to blend in and now you're going to take it all away and make me feel like an outsider again."

"No, I promise you not. If anything, I will help you see the most beautiful side of this city that you could never have done on your own."

"Iyad, I'm not looking for love. Love is too hard."

"Love is always too hard. That is what makes it so extraordinary. But I promise you, if that is what you want, then neither one of us will fall in love with the other. But you will come to love me; that I cannot help."

I turned around and stuck my hand out. "I'm Zena, and I promise never to fall in love in with you," I said.

"Hello young Zena," he said, "I am Iyad and I promise never to fall in love with you."

After the buildings fell, I put up a wall between myself and the city. I felt that I had died all over again. After the buildings fell, Iyad disappeared. He slept all day and worked all night. Picking up rubble. Inhaling toxic fumes. Looking for survivors. Looking for his people that he loved so much. Looking for New Yorkers as if they were his family. I guess to him, they were. All eleven million of them. His heart took over. His mind switched off. He could no longer take the questions of how, how, how something like this could happen? His two worlds collided. After hiding away for so many years, it all caught up with him. Violence, it seemed, was becoming universal.

As he dug away with his bare hands he questioned his identity. Arab, Arab-Amreekan, Amreekan, Earthling? He looked down at the blood on his hands as he tore away rock after rock, steel and wire shrapnel, looking for survivors. Was it his blood or theirs? Was it his blood mixed with the ashes of devastation? Was there any difference? What was he going to say to his neighbors? How was he going to explain things? Because, suddenly after September 11, 2001, all Arabs were expected to explain themselves. What if we didn't know? What if it had nothing to do with us?

I remember the day I began to love Iyad. We were sitting in his tiny apartment somewhere between SOHO, NOHO and god knows, drinking sage tea. I'd been working late in the studio and decided to stop by for a visit. I found him in his chess store, behind the counter, talking to a client who was trying to decide between a chessboard based on *The Simpsons* or a *Lord of the Rings* version. I stared through the window trying not to laugh. It was 1:00 AM and I could already guess how interesting the conversation must have been between them. The client wore a beige raincoat and looked like Colombo; which was strange since Iyad was a huge Colombo fan. What if this was him in the flesh? I walked into the store and pretended to look around. Iyad purposefully ignored me. I picked up chess pieces from different boards and examined them in the light pouring in from the street lamp.

The man in the coat looked back at me, and suddenly shifted his position, hunching over the chess sets on the counter. I noticed that he wore shiny black lace-up shoes that were wet. It wasn't raining outside and it hadn't rained all week so my curiosity peaked. His voice grew quiet and he began to talk quickly, as if trying to close the deal. I pushed my way up to the counter and looked straight into Iyad's eyes and asked him how much *The Simpsons* set cost.

"It is too pricy for you, young miss."

"I don't care," I replied, "I asked you a question."

"D-d-d-idn't you hear him," the man in the coat stammered, turning around to face me. Sadly I realized he wasn't Colombo. "You should just leave," he said pointing at the door.

"Leave? Why should I leave? It's a free country, ain't it?" Oh how I always dreamed of saying that line.

"Look, I was here first and this is my set. In fact, I already paid for it," he said pulling out a wad of dollars from inside his coat pocket. He counted out twenty crisp one-dollar bills. "There, done, go screw yourself, I told you this was my set," he exclaimed, grabbed the set and stormed out.

Iyad and I burst out laughing. I had never seen anything so strange in my life.

"You see, young Zena, this is why I sleep all day. Daytime is so boring. It is at night when New York comes to life. And speaking of night, it is almost slipping away. Come on, let's get out there and have an adventure."

"You and your adventures. I am tired. I just want to sleep."

"No, no, you can't sleep tonight. Tonight, we are going to Brooklyn to buy groceries and have a feast."

"Groceries, who is awake at this time to sell us groceries?"

"Young Zena, you think I am the only Arab in New York City who lives in an alter reality. There are many of us here, including yourself, although you probably don't wish to acknowledge it. By nightfall, the pain and burden of being away from home is too great. We cannot sleep. Our guilt takes over and we have to find any way that we can to help pass the night away. Come and see for yourself. You think you are different from us. You prance around using your studio as an excuse. Why did you stop by now and not go home? You know that conversations with me are never less than three hours long. So, don't pretend you don't know what I am trying to say."

I groaned, but nodded my head. He was right; he was always right, "OK, OK, let's go. But I have class tomorrow at 9 AM. You have to make sure I am on time."

In a second, he turned the store over to an assistant who had been sleeping in the back room, and we were off. I walked out to the curb and attempted to hail a cab. Iyad pounced on me, bringing my hand down.

"What? I'm trying to get a cab. You don't expect us to take the subway at one in the morning."

"Young Zena, we have the whole night ahead of us and a beautiful city to explore. Why waste a single moment of it? Why speed things up? We are going to walk to Brooklyn. It's not about the destination, it is about the journey."

"Are you crazy? Walk all the way to Brooklyn???"

By the time we were on the Brooklyn Bridge, it had only been forty minutes. Time literally flew. "Zena, in order to truly see a city, you have to walk it. You have to see it with open eyes. You cannot be in a hurry. You have to savor every corner you turn because you will never turn it the same way again."

I found myself being able to keep up with his pace even though I was way past exhaustion. The moon burnt brightly, leading us, protecting us. Not once did I feel unsafe. Yes, it almost felt like home. As we crossed the magnificent wooden bridge, I kept peering over the edge into the water. The whole city was reflected. I had never seen it like this before. It was truly beautiful, and somehow, it seemed to belong completely to me.

After the bridge, we took a right and slowly made our way towards Atlantic Avenue. It was there that the city came to life again. Shops were open for business. Cafes lining the streets bustled with customers. Men in long *galabiyas* sat smoking *nargilehs.* Iyad occasionally stopped to greet people, kissing them three times on their cheeks, as is the Lebanese custom. But they weren't all Lebanese. There were Algerians and Yemenites. There were Syrians and Sudanese. I stood and stared and no one seemed to take notice of me. Everyone was drinking tea and chatting away. Was I still in New York?

After what seemed like a thousand handshakes and a million kisses, we made our way to a store enshrouded by an aroma of spices. Iyad, with a huge grin on his face, shoved a plastic shopping basket towards me and instructed me to buy whatever I wanted. We were on a shopping spree and I was not to hold myself back.

"Iyad, how are we going to carry all this stuff home?"

"Where there is a will, there is a way," he said, pointing at my backpack. "Don't worry, I will carry it," he proclaimed as he grabbed it off my shoulders. If there was one thing I remember the most about Iyad, it was his brute strength. Maybe that is what happens when you live alone for so long, you forget how to touch people.

Like King Kong, his hugs always compressed all the air out of my lungs, his handshakes, crushing.

We loaded up on Arabic food that we couldn't usually buy at regular stores, paid, and then made our way back to his apartment. The walk back this time went even quicker. I was so excited and couldn't stop talking about what I'd seen. I was so happy feeling like I could finally belong in this city. All I'd needed was a little something to remind me of home, and now I had it. A small gesture that could take me one step closer to the family I left behind. I wondered about all the other people living in this great city. Did they also have their respective outlets? They must. They must have. This is how we survive. Chinatown. Little Italy. It all made sense now. I had only thought of them as tourist traps before, but now I knew how real and necessary they were.

By the time we were back at the store, the moon had gone to sleep and the lights had been turned off and the shutters were down. It was already 4:00 AM.

We kept walking until we got to the apartment. Iyad let me in first. He always did that. It was something I loved. His black shirt and tattered jeans were just a cover up for the knight that lived inside. He was a real live poet. As I squeezed through the door of his apartment, my left elbow gently pressed against his arm. His thick curly hairs tickled. It made me feel safe.

"Sit, sit," he demanded. "I will take care of everything. Study if you have to. Whatever, just don't touch a thing."

In his little kitchen, I sat down on a small wooden chair, bent over the table, placed my hands under my head, closed my eyes and fell asleep. In the background, I could hear Iyad scurrying around, opening cupboards, closing cupboards. I heard him stuff things in the fridge. I heard him receive a phone call from home.

I heard the melancholy in this voice. It broke my heart. For four hours I didn't move. Until Iyad placed his warm hand on my cheek to wake me up.

At first I was panicked. Not really knowing where I was or how I got there, but then last night's memories came flooding back. The moonlight trek to Brooklyn. The supermarket.

"Here, drink this," he said shoving a cup of steaming hot tea in my hands. "It is sage and black tea. I think you'll like it."

"Eat," he said thrusting tiny bowls full of cheese, *labneh* and olives towards me.

He ripped the bread in half. "Take," he said. "Honey? For your tea?"

Bleary-eyed and fascinated by this spectacle, I lowered my head down and whispered, "Thank you."

"You have one hour until class. Eat."

"Thank you, Iyad. Thank you."

We sat quietly sipping sage tea. Like a couple that had been married for over fifty years, we were comfortable in our silence.

Until I broke it. "Iyad, am I allowed to love you without falling *in love* with you?"

"Young Zena, you can do whatever you like. It is a free country."

We smiled at each other. I loved him. I loved him for breaking my illusions of this city. All this time, I had been trying to become New York and in one night, it all finally happened.

As I left his apartment and headed to class, I looked around me and wondered if that is how it happened to everyone else. We all come to this city as strangers, but at some point we become family, and when that transition happens it is a beautiful rebirth. To feel like you are part of the greatest city on Earth.

But after the buildings fell, I packed up my bags, and threw away my art. I said goodbye to Brooklyn, Queens and Manhattan, and I flew back to Beirut.

I left New York.

I left Iyad.

I came to Beirut. It was suicide and bliss.

SUBJECT: Are You OK???
To: zena
Fri, 7/14/06   7:11AM   1KB

Zena,
I just read that Israel dropped bombs in Lebanon. Zena are you OK? I'm worried … please tell me that you are fine. Is your family alright?
Love Marika

But before New York and Iyad, there was Maya and Beirut. The two great love affairs of my present life. And here is where my story, finally, really begins.

I met Maya on the first day of classes at the Amreekan University of Beirut in October 1994. I had just moved from Nigeria, where I had lived all of my present life so far, to start my undergraduate program in Beirut. Moving from Africa to the Middle East was not as difficult as I had imagined it would be. I went from one Amreekan school system to another. These incubators exist all around the world in order to groom us for their New World order. I believe that the sign of healthy despotism is when you're in it without even realizing it.

It was a hot and humid Arabian afternoon. Arabian afternoons are like chocolate ice cream stains on the corner of your mouth. They are sweet and sticky. They are jasmine, in bloom. My thick hair stuck to my face as I frantically ran around campus looking for my building. At that time, I still wore jeans. Today, I can't stand them; today, I only wear linen. They hung loose around my waist and were ripped at the bottoms, trailing behind my navy blue Doc Martins with the white daisies I had painted on them. It was kind of a fad, I guess. Not in Lebanon though, but somewhere far away called Seattle.

My backpack swished back and forth as I ran, irritating the small of my back that was drenched in Arabian sweat. Arabian sweat smells like orange blossoms and car exhaust. I was worried that my bra would show through my white T-shirt. There were always so many things I never cared about, but my breasts and anything that had to do with them always embarrassed me. It's not that they were too big or too small. They were just breasts.

As I walked into the moldy Arts and Sciences building in search of my history class, the stench of old books and aging professors crept into my nostrils. The color of the walls – a yellow ochre – stung my eyes. The classrooms did not have walls separating them from the main corridors, but rather decaying Arabesque cement *musharabiyehs*. The corridors had strange names that were neither Arabic nor English. Maybe it was the language of Formica. And old fava beans.

From down the hallway I heard a deep voice speaking in English with a strong Arabic accent. The words "*exam*" and "*Kaiser*" caught my ear. History had found me. Trying to catch my breath, I caught sight of a girl with long dark hair grossly entranced in what looked like a trashy romance novel. She sat straight, but with a slight hunch between her shoulders, as if to protect the sacred book she held delicately between her fingers.

I laughed to myself thinking about how much this girl reminded me of myself. This unabashed bookworm was not afraid to let her professor know that five minutes into his lecture, she was already bored. She was reading right through his introductory speech and it seemed as if she definitely had a problem with authority. I thought it was an extraordinary sight. A lot of the Lebanese girls I had met so far were not really into reading. In my eyes, they were *fashionista* zombies addicted to orange lipstick. Curious, I made my way over to the classroom hoping to make out the title of her book. I was just so intrigued. Or had I already found my refuge? She was reading in English, I noticed, from left to right. I stood in the hallway staring at her, but without my glasses on, I could not make out the title of the book.

They say that when you first meet a soul-mate, you know it right away, but it takes a while for your conscious mind to register it. I think I knew that I had just found the person who was going to become my best friend, but I was so intent on discovering the title of the book that I failed to notice the ray of sunlight that had climbed in through the *musharabiyeh* and was now bouncing off her hair.

Like a halo.

"El Kkkhalil?" a sonic boom with a thick accent resonated through the classroom, "you are late, get in."

I lowered my head to the floor and walked towards the back of the room, my thumbs curled around the straps of my army green backpack. As I passed by the girl with long dark hair and porcelain skin, she did not even bat an eyelash. She didn't even notice the pin on my bag. The one that read "FUCK AUTHORITY" or the other one, "SALAM, SHALOM, PEACE." The woman was clearly lost in a drama elsewhere. I wished I could be there too.

How I resented that university and all its backwardness. *There be monsters on campus*. It was 1994 and the civil war had ended only three years before. Prior to the war the university was rated top in the Middle East; it was a cultural hullabaloo where sexy, dark-skinned men courted blonde foreigners. It was the '60s, the "golden years" in Lebanon. Students, like others around the world, spent their time smoking hash, partaking in coitus and instigating revolution.

The revolution of the mind, that is. When the war started, all the blondies left Lebanon, so did the top professors and students, along with the credibility of the university. All that was left behind was a dull mix of shortsighted political activists who weren't old enough to vote and boxes and boxes of blue ink Bic pens. Student councils turned into militia battlegrounds. The chapter on evolution was ripped out of biology books. The word Israel was crossed out of every map and book in the library. By 1994, all that was left were expired professors, with grotesque teeth, who should have retired decades ago. The civil war had succeeded in sheltering their incompetence and secured them tenure. And I was stuck with the damage.

I could have gone anywhere in the world; London, Paris, Timbuktu. But I chose Beirut. When all the high school kids were applying for colleges, seven to ten applications each, I filled out only one. It was Beirut or bust. I had visited Lebanon several times in my childhood and always hated it. I hated the heat. I hated the traffic. I hated the incessant car honking. I hated the *kaak* vendors on the street straddling their sweaty bicycles. I hated the migrant Syrian construction workers who always tried to cop a feel. I hated the fact that I could not speak the language, Arabic or French. Hated the fact that people would pinch my cheeks, tell me how fat I was and then assure me that one day I would find a husband willing to see past my weight and lack of social skills. One that may even put up with my reading, drawing and social withdrawal. One that would teach me Arabic through his kisses and caresses.

Why go there? Why choose to move to Beirut at the prime of my youth? Beirut in 1994 seemed to be nothing but a decayed and rotten city, abandoned by God. As I filled out my college application, I felt that it was something that I just had to do. My friends told me I was crazy and demanded to know why I was giving up on life so soon. I had everything, why throw it away? But I didn't see it like that – I really believed that I had to move to Beirut. It was something deep and internal. It was my time. Little did I know Beirut had already laid her finger on *me*. I was trapped under her spell and I had no idea. She told me to come and I obeyed.

Passing by the desk of the dark-haired girl, I stole a glance at the title of her book. I knew this was the woman who would console me from the silly boyfriends who'd break my heart. This was the woman with whom I would share the secrets of losing my virginity. This was the woman who would share her version of Beirut with me, opening my eyes to her world of middle-class Sunni frenzy and the fabulous stories that went with it. The secrets, the lies, the spouse swaps, the clairvoyants and coffee ground readers. This would be the woman who would teach me vernacular Beirut.

I walked past her desk and sat down two rows behind her. I began to dream about our future adventures together. About the progressive changes we would make in our decrepit society. About the daisies we would pick. About our children, to whom we would bestow silly names, and who would become best friends and grow up to marry each other. About how we would stay up all night plotting and planning our dreams. How we would use art to change life.

Maya was going to show me the ins and outs of post-war Beirut. Her hair then was dark brown, bordering on black. Her eyebrows, massive. Her thumbs, round and wide, like her mother's and grandmothers, I'd later learn. She wore an unflattering brown jacket with a thin scarf that hung loose around her neck.

She was reading *The Age of Innocence*.

dear beirut,

> *The minute I heard my first love story*
> *I started looking for you, not knowing*
> *how blind that was.*
> *Lovers don't finally meet somewhere.*
> *They're in each other all along.*
>
> Jelaluddin Balkhi (Rumi)

6

The period after the Lebanese civil war was one of hope and change.

As of 1991, people began to rebuild their lives. They demolished and reconstructed buildings. They bought computers and cell phones. They put their energy into new faiths and systems, like corporations and loans. War was out, and a new industry was shaping itself. People grew and built, and all under the shady hand of Syrian interference in Lebanese government.

I did not see the re-birth, however. I could only see the scars. Beirut homes and buildings riddled with bullet holes. Clothing stores that were still selling bellbottoms because they had been in a twenty year coma. The cloud of hashish that covered the sky. Electricity wires that criss-crossed the city. Pirated cable. Traffic. Traffic. Traffic. I saw the alcoholics, who had lost their childhood to the war. I saw families trying to deal with depression. Families, for whom war had become a way of life, struggling to fit into the new consumer-oriented society.

The televisions told them to buy, but they had no money. People who used to stand in line for bread, now stood in line for social security; they wanted the government to pay them for the homes they'd lost. And after standing in line for hours and hours, the government always told them to come back and try again next week. This charade was to go on for years. Children who could only speak Arabic tried to understand the language and culture of the Western kids, who were returning to their homeland with their families after a twenty-year absence. Girls who were competing for the attention of boys because suddenly there was an imbalance in the ratio of men to women in the country. I saw many products once banned for being on the "blacklist" were slowly making their way back into the market. Blacklists only work during times of war, when people are convinced that they are fighting for truth and justice. But enter money and wealth and job opportunities, and people can forget so easily the brand names they swore they would never buy. The brand names that represented the oppressors. The brand names that had factories in Israel. The brand names that were associated with Zionism, like Levi's jeans, Nestlé and Coca-Cola. So many things were banned, but now, people wanted to be upright and capitalistically correct.

It was now OK to buy Coca-Cola, but it was not OK to listen to Nirvana. There was a new conspiracy brewing in the air. Kids were being taken in by the secret service and interrogated because they wore black and listened to heavy metal. Were they Satan worshippers? Did they serve the Devil? Did their music tell them to serve the Devil? Did Nirvana order them to jump out of hospital windows? My friend Milad did. Milad was a sensitive soul who could not take on Beirut. He was just one of her many victims disguised as a disturbed teenager. His hair, soft like his voice. We miss him. He was the first of many of my friends who would concede to Beirut. His mom blamed it on the music he listened to. The police investigated and compiled a list of all the music CDs in his room. There was now an official ban on close to 50 bands. The list included Oasis.

And then there were the men and women who were abused as children. And the repercussions that showed up in their day-to-day behavior as adults. During war, violence is manifested in so many ways. A caring uncle could, overnight, turn into a raging beast with an unlimited desire to fuck. His niece. His nephew. Or even his own children. These things and more are difficult to control during times of war. And when war ends, hideous crimes often go unpunished. And the children grow up with a heavy burden and an innate desire to inflict pain upon themselves and possibly, more so probably, do the very same thing that was done to them.

I saw buildings being covered in green and gray scaffolding. The cement jungle was being rebuilt. The war was being erased. Plastic and glass were in. Silicon replaced reality. The same way the buildings were being remade, so were her citizens. Girls were breaking off their cultural noses and replacing them with Barbie ones. Women, who couldn't always afford to, were inflating their breasts to help them float better in try-hard richy-rich beach resorts that were owned by former militia warlords, now turned politicians.

In *la vie en rose*, our people were drowning.

Just like their buildings, the people were becoming sexy and alluring on the outside, but hollow and empty on the inside. You had to look good. It was the only way. People were so humiliated and broken from the war, the only thing they could do was to forget. And, forgetting, it seems, was also the easiest way to deal with things. And there were at least a million and one ways to be able to forget in Lebanon. There were prescription drugs, there were over-the-counter drugs, and there were just plain-old-drugs. There was Lexotanil and Xanax. Dewars and White Horse. Lebanese Blond and Lebanese Red. Thai massages and Romanian prostitutes. There were nightclubs and super-nightclubs.

A nightclub, or simply a *night*, is where you could go to dance and drink. They usually had a predominantly male audience, because it was somehow considered shameful for a woman to go out late at night and drink and party. The difference between a nightclub and a super-nightclub was that in a super-nightclub, you could drink and dance and hook up with a "prostitute" dancer. Because, technically, prostitution is illegal, prostitutes entered Lebanon with work papers labeling them "artists" or "dancers". Everyone, from the government to immigration, knew they were prostitutes, but it was one of those things that was just allowed to happen. Typically Lebanese in nature – Lebanon always welcomes all types of people in all walks of life. We were well known for our hospitality. Prostitutes, militiamen, corrupt politicians, puritanical evangelists, poets, artists, nihilists, dreamers, writers, jihadists, businessmen – all are welcome. We were the Paris of the Middle East.

That was correct.

We had rules, rest assured. But nobody followed them.

It's funny because the practice of women coming to Lebanon for sex still happens today, only now we also hear the story in reverse. Women come to Lebanon to sleep with Lebanese men. Only this time, the women are from neighboring Arab countries, not Eastern Europe. These princesses, who have to share a husband with ten other princesses, fly to Lebanon to have their libidos satisfied. And they pay handsomely. Lebanon: a bed for everyone. Satisfaction for all. Twenty-four-seven.

While a large portion of our population was trying to forget, there were those who, try as they may, could not forget. Could never forget. These were the families who no longer had homes. Who watched brothers and sisters die in front of their eyes. Who had no money, no jobs, and no countries to which they could emigrate. The rich were getting richer and the poor, poorer. Those who could not forget – who were not allowed to forget, began to stand out. You could see it on their faces, in their clothing, and even in their salads. Iceberg was only for the rich.

In their homes, hung framed photographs of family martyrs they lost in the war. Which war? All of them. They lost count. They became angry and lost faith in the new government, and put their faith, instead, in the old militias of the war. The new government failed to supply drinking water to their homes. The new government failed to supply electricity to their neighborhood. The new government in so many ways totally disregarded a large portion of the society. And so the people put their faiths back into their militias. If the government could not rebuild their homes, the militias could. If the government could not build a school, the militias could. If the government failed to build a hospital, the militias succeeded. Soon, they had built their own community, their own country. The militias.

After the civil war ended, I saw the marginalization of Palestinians in refugee camps. I saw how people wanted to forget about them. I saw how people blamed them for everything that had gone wrong in Lebanon. And slowly they began to disappear from the reality of people's minds. And the cement walls around them grew higher and higher, isolating them from the rest of the country. Their situation was not taken up by the government. The government refused to acknowledge them, refused to grant them social services. Restricted them from getting jobs or gaining citizenship. And now they sit there, in their holding cells called "camps", with no identity, no hope, no future, no electricity, no water, no schools, no fresh air, and very little sky. Just sitting and waiting and hoping to one day return to their homeland. Generations of children have now been born right here in Lebanon, but they too only dream of going home. They live in squalor and poverty but their hearts burn bright with pride and they are filled with a firm belief that their lives in these camps are temporary. They believe in Palestine. They believe that they come from a great nation. And they believe they will return.

My sister, Lana, worked in the camps for many years. She was young and Red. She knew that these were a people who had been terribly wronged. With her hands, she helped build houses for them; with her voice, she soothed young children by telling them stories of a time better than this one. With her heart, she met Jihad.

Jihad was considerably younger than her. His eyes were bright green and his skin golden. Jihad fell in love with Lana at first sight. Her long, flowing, sun-kissed hair symbolized a freedom he could only dream about. She was not afraid of the future. She was a volunteer teacher giving an art therapy course to young children. In her free time, she carried cinder building blocks with her bare hands, sometimes two at a time, and helped build the much-needed homes. She had a dog that followed her around everywhere she went. She spoke a broken Arabic.

Lana fell in love with Jihad over time. She was considerably older. Towards the evening, she would sneak him out of the camp in her car and they would cruise Beirut. She showed him the sea, and he told her about a Palestine he had only visited in his dreams.

Together, they spoke of the future. Of how things were going to change because it just couldn't keep going on like it was, forever. Lana soon met Jihad's family, and she became like a daughter to them. Whenever anyone was sick, she brought medicine from Beirut. If it was a new year at school, she bought the schoolbooks. During Ramadan, she sat with them at their table. They would not start eating until Lana had her fair share. They always insisted she ate first. This is what they called *karam*, or hospitality. What little food they had, they could only think about giving away. This was their pride. Though they lived in an overpopulated cement jail, though open sewers surrounded them, a guest was always king (or queen) in their home. One could not weigh heavily on the present, because it was not always going to be like this. One day, they would be back in their homes. One day, they would have their land again. They have an unshakable faith.

However, this was just one of the many stories that happened in the camps. There were families who lost their faith. Who became so used to handouts, that they even stopped working. Who expected people to give up their lives for them, because they were the ones who had been wronged. And only them. They became bitter. Their eyes grew cloudy. They could not remember Palestine. They didn't care. They also wanted to forget. But how does one forget when locked behind a concrete wall? How does one forget, when all around are signs of destitution? It seemed the easiest way to forget was to simply shift to something else. To pick up a new cause. A new passion. And with time, these camps became breeding grounds for new political parties, new militias and new wars. All this while the country was regaining its status as the pearl of the Middle East. Lebanon was, and always will be, the mistress of hysteria.

Lebanon was, and always will be, schizophrenic.

While the Palestinians were being "contained", the economy was growing. The government blinded people into believing that stability had finally found Lebanon. There was a lot of work, but not enough at the same time. It was odd. No one wanted to work the low-end jobs. No one wanted to be a construction worker or garbage collector. To them, these jobs were shameful. Everyone wanted to be a banker or merchant. So after a while, the men, who survived years of civil war, and had gained titles and status, now found themselves answering the seductive call of emigration. And in their place came Syrian and Sudanese migrant workers.

One day coming home from university, Maya and I came face to face with a young boy. He was short, stocky and tan. His clothes, tattered and paint riddled, revealed that he was most probably a construction worker from a nearby building site. He was leaning against a wall, and I noticed that he was eying us. I didn't think much of it. Had I known what was to happen with him, I would have grabbed Maya and walked in the opposite direction. But this is Beirut, always full of surprises, always hurting you when you least expect it.

Maya, feeling a little down about a recent break-up, was telling me about how it was getting harder and harder to meet men in Beirut. She was practically stomping and her backpack swung from side to side. Her voice cracked; she was trying hard not to cry.

"Really Zena, I can't take it anymore. Can you believe he actually told me that he comes as a package with his friends? What do I want with them? They are all druggies. Why do I have to hang out with those fucked-up miserable people? I just want him alone. Why can't he see that they are all losers. Do you think he's a druggie too?"

"Maya, you shouldn't be upset that you didn't compromise your beliefs. You should be proud of yourself." I shifted the heavy portfolio I was carrying to my other hand so that I could walk closer to her.

"Whatever. It doesn't mean anything. I just feel so humiliated." She looked down, trying to hold the tears back. For Maya, there was nothing worse than crying in public. We walked in silence for a few seconds.

"Who cares about him," I smiled warmly. "You are going to meet someone who is going to treat you like a queen. I know it." I was about to turn around and hug her when suddenly I felt something warm and hard on my crotch.

It was a hand. I screamed.

It didn't let go.

Maya began to kick him, but he pushed her away. He was so young. How was it that he was also so strong?

"*Yeslamli hal kess*, how sweet is your cunt." He practically spat in my ear. He smelled like sweat and dust. He smelled sour.

I swung my portfolio at him, screaming and crying. His hand was still there. His grip was so tight. I could feel his fingers trying to press inside me. It was all happening so quickly. His thumb pushed hard against my pubic bone. I pushed away; he didn't let go. It hurt so much.

And then as suddenly as it started, it ended. I heard a thudding crack. Maya had seized him by his collar and thrown him against the wall. His head hit full on. His shirt ripped.

He took off and ran. There were bloodstains on the wall. Maya was holding the collar of his shirt.

I fell down. I fell into Maya's arms. My shirt was ripped. My artwork strewn all over the street. Taxis were honking. My artwork fell victim to Beirut traffic. Between my legs, it stung. It was throbbing painfully. I was almost afraid to look down. I imagined that he ripped off my privates and ran away with them.

"Fuck him," I cried. "Fuck, fuck, fuck him." I could barely breathe. I heaved and screamed. The reality of what just happened was settling. I felt pathetic. There on the ground. Near the rusty green garbage bin. On a corner in dirty Beirut. I was so embarrassed. I felt betrayed by Beirut. How could she send someone like him to me?

"Zena, are you OK? I'm so sorry. Are you OK? Are you OK?"

"No. No. No." I pushed myself to stand up. My knees were weak. It felt as if I had been raped a thousand times. "I want to kill him! I am going to kill you!" I tried to run after him.

Forgetting the portfolio, Maya held me up and we both ran. She grabbed my hand and pulled me forward. She was always the faster runner. "Let's go get him. Let's kill that fucking bastard." She still had his shirt collar in her hand.

We ran. And we ran. We ran all around Beirut. Crying. We ran through militia neighborhoods. Blue walls for one party. Green logos for another. Yellow banner for a third. Screaming. We ran through Hamra Street. Everyone stared. No one asked. Maybe such scenes have become common here. We ran down to the sea. I remember something that happened a week ago. I was in a bar having a drink with a friend, when suddenly the couple sitting next to us got into a fight. I had no idea how it started, but the woman began to scream hysterically. In the middle of the bar. No one said anything. No one got up to ask if she was OK. Then he hit her. He punched her straight in her nose. She bled and screamed and still no one got up. Not even me. This is Beirut. A mad hatter's party.

We never found him.

Giving up, we sat down on the curb of the Corniche facing the sea. It was rush hour. Cars, desperate to get home, covered us in dust. We didn't care. I was dizzy, almost in a trance, breathing so hard from crying and running so much. My tears had left streaks on my face. Maya sat right next to me. She didn't say a word. She didn't have to. She didn't try and make me get up. We just sat. In silence. In the middle of the traffic. In between my legs, it still throbbed.

"Zena, Maya? What are you doing?"

We looked up. It was Firas in his car. We had broken up only two months before. He called it quits. I was too much for him. I was too emotional. He cheated on me.

Was this all Beirut could throw at me?

I wanted to tell him to keep driving, that nothing would make me get into his car. But sometimes we have to stand a little more humiliation before we can be strong again. We got in. He drove us home. In silence. We didn't have to tell him what had happened. He knew that it was something big. Something horrible. He didn't ask. He just let us sit.

In silence.

Firas, thank you for not asking on that day.

7

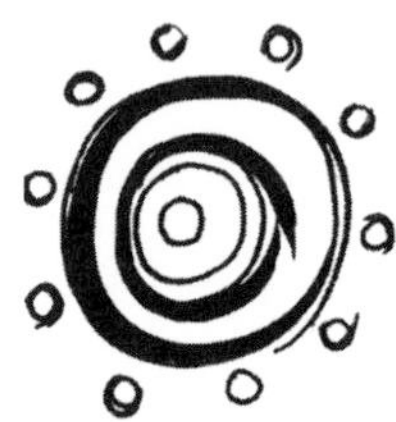

In the year 2000, the Israelis withdrew after having occupied the south of Lebanon for twenty-two years.

Because of the occupation, until the year 2000, I had gone through my entire life without ever having visited the village of my ancestors, Hasbaya. The village where my Grandpa Mohammad and my father grew up.

My Grandpa Mohammad built our house in Hasbaya on top of a hill. It was a typical two-floor Lebanese-style village home. The façade was covered in cut limestone squares and the roof consisted of red shingles. The kitchen, dining room, and living room were on the lower floor. The upper floor was divided into three rooms. One for Mohammad and his wife. One for the two girls . And the other for the six boys. Talking to my father today, his fondest memories always take him back to the summers they spent in Hasbaya.

He says that it was there that he learnt to become a man.

Hasbaya taught my father how to be strong and courageous. Hasbaya taught him how to defend his faiths and beliefs. It was there that he bonded with his brothers and discovered the importance of family values. It was during the long hot and dry days that his endurance and vigor were tested. But most importantly, it was there that he spent dreamy nights under their majestic oak tree, listening to Baba Sami, Grandpa Mohammad's brother, tell tales of brave Druze warriors of the past. My father came to define himself through these stories.

In the early '70s my Grandpa Mohammad had begun constructing a new and more modern house across from the older one. His family was growing and he wanted to make sure he could build in order to pass on real estate to his sons. The apartment complex was three floors high and built in concrete. He prided himself in the vision of his sons and their future families all living in the same building. His family was everything to him. After years of working in Mexico and Africa, he felt that he had finally earned the right to settle down and watch his family grow.

Later that decade, fighting erupted in Lebanon. The Palestinian Liberation Organization (PLO) had been fighting their guerilla war on Israel from the south of Lebanon, in hopes of taking back their country. The PLO, for a while, settled into our home. A few weeks later, Israeli jet planes blew up our building. The PLO retreated to another location.

My Grandpa, determined to build his dream home for his family, began to reconstruct. He poured the concrete and built the skeleton of the building for the second time. The year was 1982. The Israeli army officially took control of the entire South Lebanon region and my Grandpa's building project halted once again. The occupiers deduced that our quaint little village home was a strategic military point. They moved in and took over. Their blue and white flag was strung up and our home was transformed into their main headquarters for that area. There is a perfect 360-degree view of the entire region from that hill.

Because of the occupation my grandfather was never able to

return to Hasbaya again or finish his dream home. Grandpa Mohammad passed away in 1993. It would be seven more years until the Israeli army would leave our home.

The occupiers finished building the home my Grandpa started. Except, instead of providing rooms for a growing family, they built interrogation booths, holding cells, torture rooms, and of course, bureaucratic offices. Right next to our oak tree. Right on top of the very same building they had blown up only a few years before.

Directly under our oak tree, they built a bunker in which they slept. The roof of this bunker was around two meters of reinforced concrete. Nothing could penetrate that roof. It was the safest spot in South Lebanon.

I know all this because the day after the Israelis pulled out of South Lebanon, my entire family drove down to our home: cousins, aunts, and uncles. It had been almost twenty years since an el Khalil set foot on that land. We all tried not to cry. After all, it should have been a day to rejoice. It was May 25, 2000, which has come to be known as Liberation Day.

We barely realized that we had arrived. My father and uncles did not recognize the plot of land at first. Even their beloved oak tree was disguised by the hideous bunker.

Silence.

There was a lot of silence.

We solemnly stepped out of the cars and each began to walk around in different directions. My father went straight to the old house. My brother and I decided to explore the larger concrete building. We didn't know it was a relatively new construction.

I guess it's a good thing Grandpa Mohammad was not alive to see this.

Nadim and I walked into the building. I stood at the doorway for a few minutes, not quite ready to step inside. Waiting for my eyes to adjust to the dim light, I scanned the entrance of the building. It was dark and humid. And completely empty. The walls were a yellowish gray and heavily stained with dirt and what seemed to be remnants of cigarette smoke. Straight in front of me was a small window, the only light source. I opened the door a little wider to allow in more light.

Nothing. It was totally abandoned.

The floor was filthy; soiled by brown footprints. It looked like whoever moved out did so in quite a hurry. I grabbed Nadim's hand and we both stepped in together. It was as if we were twelve years old again. We crossed through the entrance and made our way to the right, towards the staircase. I looked at Nadim. He was clearly worried, but our curiosity overpowered our fear, and led us up the staircase. Our steps were slow and calculated. I kept wondering if there were any explosives or traps that may have been left on the stairs. It was very hard to see anything.

Somehow, nothing exploded and we made it to the top of the staircase and onto the next floor. The purpose of the building became very clear to us as we came face-to-face with a row of metal bars.

They were holding cells.

I was almost crushing Nadim's hand. We walked towards the bars. A powerful stench filled the space. At first I was worried that it might be a dead body. I was terrified. Nadim told me to pull myself together as he pointed to the dark spots on the cell floor.

"Look, Zena, it's just shit. This whole floor is covered in shit. They didn't even give the prisoners toilets. They just let them shit on the floors."

My stomach lurched and I put my hand up to my mouth to keep myself from vomiting. "I'm sorry, Nemo", I said, calling him by his nickname, "I have to get out of here. I'm going to vomit." Letting go of his hand, I ran down the stairs and out of the building. It was too much and I had no intention of exploring the third floor above.

Outside, I found the rest of my family huddled around the oak tree. They were furious about something. I ran towards them to see what was going on.

"How are we going to get rid of this fucking bunker? The building is easy – we can just knock it down. But for this bunker ... we will have to use explosives. The roof is so thick. And if we use explosives, we'll hurt the tree. There is no way we are going to damage this tree. What are we supposed to do?"

At this point, Nadim walked out of the building and signaled me to follow him. We walked around the back and I caught Lana and younger brother Seif climbing on top of what looked to be a sniper dugout.

"There," Nadim said pointing to Lana and Seif, "from the third floor, I counted twelve of those dugouts. They completely surround the house."

"Zena, Zena, look at this ... this is so funny." Seif pointed to the cement walls of the dugout. They were all completely covered in scribbles and drawings. I was puzzled and leaned in for a closer look. To my horror and surprise, I found that I could actually read the scribbles. They were in English.

"Listen to this one," Seif read out loud, "top ten things I want to do when I get back home."

I edged over to him and read:

> Get laid without having to pay for it
> Never wear khaki and green again
> Watch a football game
> Eat mom's cooking

Take a hot shower
Go out for drinks with my friends

I had always wondered about the stories of Jewish Amreekan kids being flown to Israel for free. About the "youth programs" designed for them to "discover their roots". Being taken to a hippie kibbutz, a kind of summer camp, where they all sat around campfires and sang songs about Israel in Hebrew. An Israel they didn't even know. An Israel devoid of Palestinians. They were college kids and teenagers with raging hormones. They wanted to believe. They wanted to fit in. Why go back to Amreeka when you could have Mediterranean weather, citrus fruits, olive trees and Amoula's "Sexy Semites"? Why go back when you could stay and fight for your fantasy homeland? They met others like them and fell in love. They stayed. They joined the army, mandatory for both boys and girls. They fought. They fought for a land they could never truly know, because from the very first moment they stepped on her soil, they failed to acknowledge and experience her true culture. From the very moment they were coerced to visit this Holy Land, they were conditioned with a false sense of reality. They were promised instant citizenship. And really, who could blame them? The system created to eradicate Palestinians has been exceptionally crafted. Those college kids, I don't blame them. They never stood a chance.

I looked back at Seif; he was tracing the writings on the wall with his finger, and seemed to be in a state of confusion, anger, and disappointment. For an instant, I thought about taking the conversation a step further and explaining to him the concept of an apartheid system, but decided against it. He was probably feeling shitty enough already.

"Come on guys," I said, "let's go check out the bunker under the tree."

Crossing back to the bunker, I saw that the older members of the family had walked over to the building that contained the holding cells. I wanted to yell out and tell them not to go in, but I guess it was important for them to see with their own eyes. It was a type of gruesome closure that had to happen. I put my head down and continued walking to the bunker.

At the entrance, I found a scrap of paper. I squatted down to try and read it. To my surprise, it was a drawing. A crayon drawing of two stick figures. One, a young girl with curly blond hair. The other, a tall man with a mustache. They were holding hands. On the bottom it read, "*come home soon daddy*". Again in English. It made me wonder who these soldiers really were. It was as if I was caught in some sick, warped reality. Had Amreeka really stretched its tentacles this far? Who were these people called Israelis anyway? Why were they here in my home? What on earth could convince a man to leave his young daughter behind and come and occupy my home? The reality of the situation came crashing down. An army had been supported by the greatest superpower on the planet. It took over my home. It took over my father's home. It took away the sweat and toil of my grandfather's dreams. It came. It occupied. It fucked with its neighbors. It broke our hearts. It created fear and animosity. It showed lack of respect to the land that provides them with so much. It fucked with our minds and bred fear and hatred. It came. It occupied. It sat. It shat. It shat all over my grandfather's home.

I folded the piece of paper and put it into my pocket.

Evidence.

Pulling myself together, I stood up and took a few steps inside. Straight in front of me, I saw the beds. I counted twenty-three. On the right, there was a small kitchen. What I saw next, I found very hard to explain. It was unlike anything I had ever come across before in my whole life.

The table was set for lunch. There were bowls of salad. Slices of bread. Bottles of water. Plates of tomatoes and onions. And a large tray of slightly burnt *m'jadara*. I felt like I was Snow White walking into the dwarfs' home. Great, I thought to myself, first they try to steal our falafel and claim it as their own and now they are after our bean dish. I walked closer to the table and looked at the food. It was made the same way we make ours. I wondered if their chef was a local from the village. Most probably, right?

At the end of the table, there were three large plastic bottles of Coca-Cola. The logo was in Hebrew. It was surreal to see Hebrew writing on a product in Lebanon. It was surreal, but not unbelievable. At the time, Coca-Cola was still banned in Lebanon due to its support and contribution to the Zionist state. I thought it was funny that they didn't drink our local Pepsi. Maybe it was their way of making a statement. By drinking Coca-Cola, they somehow felt like they were closer to home. It was a nationalist statement. Amazing how even consumer goods can make a political statement in Lebanon.

When the decision to pull out of Lebanon was announced, twenty-two years of Israeli occupation was dismantled in a matter of forty-eight hours. They took all evidence with them, from desks and paperwork to their captives in the holding cells. I guessed that the soldiers occupying our house were just about to sit down for lunch when they got the call. It was such a strange sight. Even the glasses were still filled with water. They didn't even get the chance to have a sip.

I remember thinking about the boy who just wanted to get laid. Maybe it was happening at this very moment. I wondered where he was: Amreeka or Israel? I remember thinking about the people in the holding cells. They were now captives somewhere else. Who were they to begin with – Lebanese or Palestinians? Where were they now – Israel or Amreeka? Would they ever see their families again? What had they done to be put into those cells in the first place? At least here, they were prisoners in their own country. Now they belong to another system, another place, with no rights and no way to get back home.

Back outside, I saw that my family had reconvened under the oak tree. There was a strange man with them now and they were all yelling at him.

"You? You built it? I don't believe this. Our families have known each other for hundreds of years. And then you go and build this monstrosity for our enemies. Here, on our sacred soil? Shame on you!"

"It wasn't my fault. If I didn't do it, they would have killed me," he pleaded.

This man was a local from a village close by. During the occupation, a lot of Lebanese were forced to work for the Israeli soldiers. Most of the work consisted of manual labor, but some were also drafted into the South Lebanese Army. This army, called *Lahed* in Arabic, was Israel's proxy army in the south. The day the occupation fell apart was the day Hezbollah soldiers, through their work as double agents, infiltrated the Middle Lahed Command, and convinced them to stop working for the Israeli army. Hezbollah promised them that there would be no revenge war against the Lahed. That they would not be held responsible, because during occupation, shit happens. On May 22, 2000 the Middle Lahed Command dropped their guns and retreated to Lebanese-controlled soil. A huge corridor was now open to the very border of Israel. The Israeli army freaked out. Within two days, all signs of the Israeli army vanished, except for the weapons they left behind.

The weapons were left intentionally. Their hopes were that the locals, the Lahed, who feared retribution, would pick up the guns to protect themselves against Hezbollah, instigating a fresh civil war. What they didn't understand was that Hezbollah really did keep their word about not having a revenge war. They picked up all the weapons and handed them over to the official Lebanese army. Lahed army soldiers were only given six months in jail. A small symbolic sentence. Hezbollah were seen as the new heroes of Lebanon. The heroes who liberated Lebanon from Israeli occupation. And the civil war never happened. And May 25, Liberation Day, became a national holiday.

The man who built the bunker under our oak tree was not a Lahed soldier, but he was one of the many civilians victimized by the Israeli occupation. He was threatened to build it or watch his family be massacred. He built it. Shit happens.

"If it's any consolation, I built it in a very special way. I know how much your family loves that tree. I had that in mind while I poured the concrete. I know how to dismantle it. We don't even have to use explosives. Trust me," he said.

It took a year before my family could start dismantling the structures that had been built on their land. Apparently during the occupation, the Israeli army planted land mines all around our hill. This was their attempt to deter Hezbollah soldiers from attacking their outpost. It took the Lebanese army a year to clear the mines. But finally one day, it was all gone.

The occupation, the mines, the prisoner shit building, the horny dugouts, the weapons, and of course the bunker.

And I can happily report that our tree, today, is alive and well.

8 

The first boy I ever slept with ended up cheating on me eight months later.

With his cousin.

It was 1995. I was eighteen years old and decided that it was finally time to become a woman. Having just moved over to Lebanon, I found that I could not assimilate into the culture when it came to the expectations of being a woman. By nature, I have always been a bit of a tomboy. Growing up in Nigeria, I used to practice karate. I even had a few medals from regional competitions. And then there was the whole disgust with breasts thing.

My new social environment in Beirut demanded that I be more feminine-looking. It demanded that girls look like girls and boys like boys. It demanded that I style my hair weekly at the hairdresser. Adorn my fingernails with bright polish. Speak softly and giggle often. Wear clothes that hugged my body, to show off my childbearing hips. No one knew how to deal with my tomboyish personality. My aunt would sigh every time I walked in with dirty sandals. My grandmother would shrug her shoulders when she saw me in torn-up jeans. And my cousins believed I was a hopeless case and that no one would ever marry me. How could anyone marry someone who only wore white baggy T-shirts?

I thought it would be much easier to skip past all the manicuring sessions, hairdresser experiences, and miniskirt indulgences, which were destined to fail with me anyway, and go straight to the point. Having sex would instantly make me a woman.

But it wasn't for practical reasons only. Somehow, I also truly believed that I was going to marry this boy. He was my first boyfriend. My first real love. And eventually, my first lover.

We met during my first few days at the university. A few months later, on the rooftop of my apartment, I told him that I wanted him to make love to me. A few weeks later, it happened. I lit candles to make it special. I put in my favorite CD. At the time it was the soundtrack to *Natural Born Killers*. The lyrics that played during the first penetration went something like this: "the only one who could ever reach me, was a sweet-talkin' son of a preacher man."

It hurt. And I cried.

But I was now a woman and that was all that mattered.

Sex with Bilal turned out to be a big scam. He never gave me pleasure. I guess we both didn't know how to figure out how to work my parts. We were young. I can't blame him. I always used to fake it because I was too shy to admit that I was feeling nothing but pain. I wanted to be like those women on TV. I wanted sex to be noisy, sweaty, and effortless.

The next few months were full of dull sex, insecurities and yeast infections. It was not anything close to what I was hoping it would be like. This was spring.

In summer, he ran into his long-lost cousin and slept with her. At first I pardoned him because he said that they were both drunk. But then he told me that they did it again in the morning.

That is when I threw up.

And even still, I could not bring myself to end the relationship with him. I was so young and full of faith. I believed that if we could get though this, we could get through anything.

Two months later I found out that he cheated on me again. I had been away from Beirut on a short trip to Nigeria. On my return, we had agreed that he would pick me up from the airport. I disembarked the plane feeling like a grown-up. Like a woman who was about to be reunited with her long-lost lover. Waiting for my bags, I looked at the other passengers wondering if they could tell if I was a virgin or not. I had planned that as I crossed into the reception area and locked eyes with Bilal that I would throw my bags down and jump into his arms, kiss him madly, maybe even tumble over, and make a real scene.

No one's arms were there to jump into.

I took a taxi and dumped my bags at home. I then walked over to his apartment. It was around eight in the morning. I rang his doorbell. Once, twice, until I heard the shuffling of feet.

He opened. He was only wearing his boxers. Still sleepy, he did not register my face.

"Hi, Bilal."

"Zena? What are you doing here?"

"I just arrived from the airport. You were supposed to pick me up, did you forget?"

"Yes! I'm so sorry."

"Can I come in? I missed you so much." I leaned over to kiss him when I noticed red and brown marks on his neck. "Bilal, what's wrong with your neck?"

"Oh, those ... this is nothing. I was fooling around with the guys and got punched in the neck. We were just wrestling around ...

they're just bruises. And then on top of all that, I cut myself shaving a few times. Don't worry, it's nothing."

How was I to know they were hickies? It was the first time I had seen such things.

Three days later, we split up.

The sad thing is that I was still willing to give him another chance.

But I have to say that had this experience not happened, I may have never gotten to know Maya well. Up until then, she was a good friend that I loved and trusted, but always from a distance. I met Bilal as soon as I moved to Beirut and our intense romance made it almost impossible for me to get close to anyone else. I always knew Maya and I were destined to become best friends, but the opportunity had not presented itself.

It was this particular disaster that sealed our friendship forever.

Up until the break-up with Bilal, I had not told anyone that I had lost my virginity. Our sleeping together had been kept a secret from Beirut, because it was such a taboo at the time. And on top of that, though he had his own apartment, he was practically living with me for several months. In Lebanon, it is illegal for two unmarried people to live together, We were only nineteen. I wanted to break all the rules.

Maya received my news very well. She asked me detailed questions about everything from the break-up to the sex. She made a doctor's appointment for me and made sure I started having regular checkups and Pap smears. She pushed me to heal myself spiritually. We exercised and ate healthily. We talked for hours about Beirut and men.

I healed perfectly.

Maya, thank you.

9

In my early years in Beirut, I was at war with the nightly *tabbal* during Ramadan. He would walk down my street every night for that month beating his drums, urging us to wake up and eat one last time before the sun came out. Every night I threw my shoe at him and told him I wasn't Muslim and that I didn't fast. He would laugh and keep drumming. Now that I think about it, I could have gotten into serious trouble, but there is something about being cuckoo in Beirut. It is a method of being that exists just for Beirut. And it is an understanding that those who live here have to put up with each other. Occasionally, and to varying degrees, we all need to put on the cuckoo mask.

Maybe it is how we survive. I love it.

Beirut is total and absolute freedom. It is imagination uncensored. What you will to happen can happen. To lose myself in her frenzy is absolute bliss, like the second orgasm that is always better than the first.

There were no strict laws at the time. People had just come out of decades of civil war and all they wanted to do was party. They created elaborate outfits from their moldy closets. They painted their cars funny colors. They smoke and drank and snorted everything they could find. We wrote poetry. We jumped over fences into abandoned houses and drank vodka under the stars. We parked on the Corniche and made out until our windows fogged and the police tapped on them, demanding to see our ID. We didn't care about being interrogated or even slapped around because love and sex and drugs and alcohol were our new law and order. They replaced sectarian violence, militia takeovers, red streaks left over in the sky by tracer ammunition, checkpoints, and extortion.

It was a big fucking celebration that has somehow carried on till today. It was a mad celebration and the reason we call it madness is because, in so many ways, the war never really ended. There were still bombings and assassinations. But we turned a blind eye, because technically, on paper, some kind of treaty had been signed; which now meant that we could come and go as we pleased in Beirut, without the fear of being shot by a sniper, blown up by a car bomb, or kidnapped because of our religious or social background. We now became best friends with Beirut and best friends with our brothers and sisters who only a year ago had their guns pointed at our faces.

And who could blame us? Despite years of civil war, foreign intervention and occupation, mass murders, genocides, and basic life in hell, we deserved a chance to breathe. Despite all that, Beirut had still managed to retain her beauty and dignity and we wanted to celebrate her. Despite years of violence, one could now walk on the street at night and never fear being mugged. Petty crime no longer existed – people were tired of it. Beirut still had her glorious sunrises that exploded over her mountains, and her splendid sunsets that plunged into her sea.

She had her mom-and-pop stores that always delivered service with love and attentiveness. She had quiet and calm reminiscent of life in a quaint village.

Being in Love in Beirut:
A list of thing that I love (in no particular order):

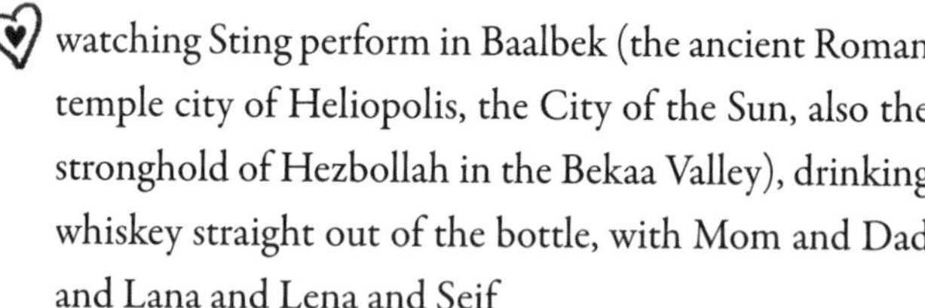

- watching Sting perform in Baalbek (the ancient Roman temple city of Heliopolis, the City of the Sun, also the stronghold of Hezbollah in the Bekaa Valley), drinking whiskey straight out of the bottle, with Mom and Dad and Lana and Lena and Seif
- the cramps I got in my leg in Hasbaya, made me sit down and realize how beautiful the mountains around me were, made a charming young man kneel down and help me stretch out my leg to get the cramp out
- listening to jazz under the stars at the ancient port city of Byblos, thinking about how as I was sitting under 7,000 years of civilization, jazz sounded really good that night
- the first time Mom met Maya's mom, Maya and I were both wearing our Doc Martins and our moms, over coffee, complained about how Maya and I needed to work on being more feminine, watching Maya wink at me when her mom shrugged her shoulders in despair
- seeing Ziad Rahbani play live, giving him Iyad's letter
- eating a *manouche*, a hot melted cheese pastry, at 6:00 AM after a night of drinking, dancing, driving fast with the top of my car down, Rayess Bek rapping about Beirut (in silence), feeling invincible
- dancing at Walimet Warde restaurant to traditional live

Arabic music, drinking lots of arak, watching the clear liquid turn white when I add water to it

- swimming, swimming in our sea, in Sour and in Batroun, swimming at night, holding my breath underwater for as long as I can
- being on the Corniche, watching the purple color that first peaks over the mountains as the sun rises
- eating a French-fry sandwich from the King of Fries restaurant on Hamra Street, with pickles and ketchup, no mayo
- drinking vodka sec, anywhere
- walking barefoot, in the sand, on hot tiles, on the soil, in a forest near the Cedars, in water, in mud, in South Lebanon
- music, listening to music really loud, in general, Arabic Hip Hop, Arabic classics, and sometimes even Arabic pop
- wine, alone, with a lover, on the beach, on my roof, on the Corniche
- fire
- Tapi
- camping
- my family
- laughing, laughter
- a great idea
- an I love you
- a back rub, a back scratch
- coming effortlessly, or sweating a lot first
- the wind in my hair
- the moon, big and strong, yellow

- my sandals, smelly, worn out from walking all around Beirut
- licking a lover's skin after a day on the Mediterranean
- raspberry sorbet, lemon sorbet
- sage tea in the winter, winter, rain, the first rainfall in Beirut, the smell of the dust
- glitter
- the almost drowning scene in the movie *The Piano* because if I were ever to describe Beirut in 30 seconds as a visual, that would be it
- hearing my neighbors having sex though the roof and walls (I am happy they are happy)
- green olives, tea and labneh for breakfast and, or dinner
- swings on balconies that overlook the Beirut cityscape
- my garden, Um Tarek's advice for my flowers, watering it at night, sitting in it at night, or in the morning, checking my email from there (cool wireless connection)
- *batata harra* (chilli potatoes) at Abu Hassan's
- Pink Floyd, while driving, while sitting on my balcony, while developing photos in the lab, in the dark, in bed with my headphones on
- Asmahan
- the morning after binge drinking, feeling like I've been reborn, like I've been given another chance to live
- Iyad
- so much
- dancing to 80s music
- disco
- Boney M's *Born to Be Alive*

- kissing
- kissing in Beirut in secret, in public, on the Corniche, on the street, in a home, on a bed, in a supermarket, in the car, on a bridge, near the border, on top of a mountain, at Palace Café, drunk in Barometre, in my car listening to Billie, in my car listening to Nina.

But I know some people who took their relationship with Beirut too far.

> Dear Firas,
> Do you remember the time you almost jumped out your window? It was during the winter solstice. You called me and told me you were sitting on your windowsill and that life no longer had any meaning. Your father was divorcing your mother and you could not stand to see her humiliated. Many years later she died of a broken heart. She never recovered. Stress brings on cancer.
>
> It was winter and you were sitting on your windowsill. I drove over to your house like a crazed woman. It felt like a Scorsese flick. The streets of Beirut were wet with rain. The traffic lights seemed to be on a permanent red. Not that it mattered because I crossed them all. Not that it mattered because we don't have traffic police here. Not that it mattered, but I never understood why they put in the lights in the first place. Are they trying to fool the western tourists who come here to visit? Do they want them to feel safe and encourage more tourists to visit simply because we have traffic lights? I remember when we didn't. Not much has changed since then.
>
> Driving to your house, I see the reflection of tragic red lights on the wet wet streets. It looked like blood. Your blood. The blood of Qana. Where Jesus turned water into wine. Where the Israelis blew up about a hundred

women and children in what was called Operation Grapes of Wrath.

water
wine
blood
rain
traffic lights

I remember how small your feet looked as I stood under your apartment building. I thought about how ridiculous you would look if you died barefoot in your boxers. I was not going to let you die like this.

Did I save you that night because I loved you or because I wanted to save you? The answer presented itself to me months later when you finally had the courage to stand up and leave me.

You were tired of being loved.

And I am just a Mother Teresa when it comes to distraught Beiruti men. I, who should be wild and boundless, find myself in the chronic comfort of troubled men. I, who should always be throwing my shoes out of windows, find myself consoling weak and frantic men. I, who should be walking the nights in tight red dresses, find myself cradling balding men as they weep in my arms.

It is really the men who deserve to cry in this city. All this pressure they are constantly under. Here in the black hole sun of the Middle East, how do you show that you have become a man? How do you cross to the other side? What do you have to do to present yourself as worthy of being called a man? What if you can't fight? What if you can't wheel and deal? What if you just want to dance?

I love you. I will always love you for not being brave enough to tell me that I was killing you. Once, you asked me to grant you one night. And when I did, you cried in my arms the whole night through. You stayed in my bed. You helped me throw shoes at the night drummer. We made love during the holy month. We drank wine. We recited Rumi and al-Mutanabbi. I pretended to be Scheherazade. We climbed up on the roof and watched the sun come up. We drank more wine and vowed that we would always stay pure. That we would always do what our hearts commanded of us. That we would walk the tightrope and never fall. That neither war, nor bombs, nor unfriendly neighbors would ever break our spirit. That love was king and I was your queen. That we would run through wet laundry under the desert sun. That every moment would be precious. That every moment would give birth to a new one. That life could be what we wanted it to be. That there would be no more planes breaking the sound barrier. That there would be no more assassinations. That there would be no restrictions. No restrictions to love. No religion, but love. That we would drive at high speeds and never crash. That we would drink and never pass out. That the stars would always guide us. That the sound of prayer from the mosque down the street was the signal for lovemaking. That climaxes would be reached before the call to prayer was over. That we would live forever, like the stencils of martyred militiamen on tattered Beirut walls. Like stray cats who always found their chicken bones. Like the sea, the endless blue. Like your eyes, an endless forever. Like bitter coffee, I swore never to write about. Like war ... that will never end. We were at war, you and I. It was us against reality. It was our madness, against black veiled nights. It was our hearts, against bullet-riddled walls. It was our souls, against the nature of man. It was love, when there should have been death. It was light, when the sea went to sleep. It was warmth, when Beirut was shot dead.

I never thought I could live it without you. I never thought I could find Beirut again after you left me.

But I did.

Because as long as there are men who need to be loved, Beirut will open her arms to me and present me with her next victim.

I love you. I always loved each and every one of you. Because you all brought me Beirut. In her full glory. In her madness unrestrained.

She shot my heart over and over. It was always a surprise. It was always an end and a new beginning. The morning after a bottle of vodka. A rebirth. Drinking water after eating ice cream. The chills of a great song. The panic attack after smoking hash. The ghosts in the tunnels. The thousands, 17,000 people to be exact, who are still declared missing. It is the undiscovered mass graves. It is the hanging that will follow. It is a hymen repair operation. It is the addiction for the next bomb. It is orange lipstick and grapevine shelters. It is riding a bicycle when you should be choosing a husband. It is wearing a wedding dress and running through the streets of Beirut. It is discovering religion through sex. It is discovering music through war. It is eating processed cheese on round flat bread. It is drinking whisky with three ices exactly.

It is crying while you sleep.

It is vomiting black flies.

It is killing while you come.

10

The period after the Lebanese civil war ended was bittersweet.

It was a time of extremes. One was either incredibly happy, incredibly sad or incredibly stoned. We happy ones did our best to rebuild the country, happily. We started NGOs and support groups. We exhibited art and published poetry. We organized architectural competitions to rebuild our city center. We counseled people who, because of the war, suffered from anxiety and depression. Despite all the odds, we tried to learn how to live as a community again. We attempted to reconcile with our pasts. We attempted to negotiate a national identity. We stayed up all night drawing plans about how we were going to rebuild our lives, and establish a consensus on trust, tolerance, and love. Despite the pressure from our neighbors, the Israelis, who constantly threatened to destabilize us. Despite the pressure of living under a new occupation – a Syrian one. We stayed up all night; we sacrificed our health, our personal dreams, in order to build a collective memory. In order to rebuild Lebanon.

And we did it with such ease. Because after years of oppression and conflict, we learn that the only thing we can do, is to stand up and move on. We Lebanese have mastered that art. We fight through the night; come day, we get up, put on our suits and head off to work ... often as if nothing happened. I don't know if this is a blessing or a curse.

Those of us who could not partake in the rebuilding, for their own personal reasons, emigrated to find work. To make money to support their broken families. To build a new life. To forget. To let go. If one were to analyze this statistically, it is clear that the majority of people who emigrated from Lebanon were men.

When our Lebanese men began to emigrate, we became conscious of their disappearance. Where were they all going? Those with dark hair and dark skin began to vanish; they said they were being welcomed in the Arabian Gulf. Those with light hair and blue eyes left the country; they said that Europe and Amreeka embraced them with open arms. Soon, there weren't enough men left for the women and it was at that point that the women began to turn to each other.

Women fell in love with women, not because they were born to do so, but because they were bored and lonely and it was easy to do so, despite the fact that, by law, in Lebanon, it is illegal to "*partake in a sexual act that goes against nature*". They held hands in public and no one noticed. They kissed in the bathrooms of nightclubs and no one cared. They spoke in code and poetry. They danced to their own rhythm. Everyone was just happy to be in love and be loved. After the war, no one wanted to follow rules. We were all tired of them.

After the war, lines were beginning to blur. Lines at the nightclubs. Lines to the bathroom. Lines of coke. We drank all night. We danced. We drove. We wrote. We loved, we made love. We found new spaces that never existed before in our beautiful country. And it was in these spaces that we created great works of art and literature that were so acerbic, they were actually beautiful. It was in these uncontrolled spaces that we gave into our innermost desires and realized that sex was only a cover for a much bigger emotional need. We learned to reconcile with ourselves and the only way to do that was to sleep with as many people as possible. By owning their bodies, we were taking ours back. We lived the war. Survived it. Our bodies were alive and the only way to verify it was to glorify it. Sex became an addiction. And with the shortage of men in the country, we shed our shame and turned to each other.

Those of us who stayed to rebuild lived intensely. We tried to talk about the war. We promised never to forget what happened. We wanted to try and learn from it. We swore to make sure that no one around us would forget. But we were already forgetting. It was an ironic situation. We worked to rebuild in the daytime, but at night, we drank to forget. We tried to stay self-aware. We fought not to become the hypocrites our parents had become.

We promised to take the money and wealth from the warmongers, now politicians, and distribute it to the masses. We walked on Hamra Street and studied the mistakes the generations before us made. The blind faith they put into dangerous idealism. The very same faith that lead them to participate in massacres and religious profiling. We swore never to be like them. We swore to find our own identities and not be swayed. Just because it worked for the French, the Amreekans or the Iranians doesn't mean it will work for us. We saw the work ahead of us and we vowed to take it head on. We vowed to create a cultural revolution that was a reality of everyday life. But paradoxically, the more vows we created, the more we broke. The more we spoke, the more we drank. The more we thought ... the more sex we had. Nothing was getting done. Nothing would. It was bodies eating bodies. We were tired.

Foreign intervention made it difficult to get anything done. Age-old feudal systems made certain changes impossible. We were young; maybe we just wanted to hang out in malls like the kids were doing in other countries. Maybe we just wanted to watch TV. Maybe we just wanted to do small and silly things. But post-war Beirut was a challenge we could not avoid. It was in our faces. It affected our lives, jobs, education, and dreams. We were young, we just wanted to live, but we didn't realize that by growing up too quickly we were also hurting each other; what we didn't do with guns, we were doing with sex. In public we voiced our opposition, but in the darkness we released our disappointments upon each other. We, the dreamers, could not keep up with the pace of the government and businessmen, who overnight signed mega-million-dollar contracts. Slow down. Slow down, we begged them. Think about how you are doing this. Think about what it means to rebuild so quickly. And realizing we couldn't keep up, we decided to live today and work tomorrow.

But in Beirut ... tomorrow never comes. In the Arab world, tomorrow can span tomorrow, next week, next year, or next century.

After the war, economic constraints found themselves present and some of us grew tired and were filled with a deep pessimism. Some of us could not fight the corporate giant that was eating our city alive and brainwashing our people, making them believe that the solution to post-war living was to buy, buy, buy. Some of us lost faith in our beliefs.

Lost sight of our dreams.

Had bitter ends with our lovers.

Where do you go when you have no love worth fighting for? Where do you go when the only thing affirming your existence are the commercials on TV urging you to buy a new refrigerator?

Everything was going wrong.

Where do you go when you want to be an artist, but realize there is no real word for it in Arabic? That if you said artist, it could be translated into "East European prostitute"? That if you said artist, people just assumed you to be a drug addict or a *hashesh*? That if you said artist, it meant that you did nothing in life, but were on the prowl for a husband? That if you said artist, it meant that you were not good at math and thus could never get a high-end job? That if you said artist, it meant that you were a floozy stuck in a dream world with no care for anything? That if you said artist, all you really wanted was to get laid? That if you were an artist, it meant you were still stuck in '70s Arab idealism? That if you were an artist, you only painted wild galloping Arabian horses and sculpted fists rising out of marble? That if you were an artist, it meant that you needed help; that people should feel sorry for you because you can't do anything else? Why would you want to be an artist when you could be a banker, lawyer, or an advertising mogul?

I grew up most of my life thinking I was invincible. That I was a descendant of *Jor-El*. But after a few years in Beirut, my spirit was tested. I had gotten too close and I was unprepared. My beautiful vampire had sucked me dry. My lovers had all left me. My fellow artists were selling themselves to the highest bidder. I was visiting the mega-hypermarkets more than my studio. My books were collecting dust. My pen had run dry. I drank. I drank. I drank.

I wanted to forget the disappointments. Wanted to find peace. Quickly.

But Beirut grew lucid. And I, afraid.

The monster began to eat the poet.

And then I fell.

I stopped sleeping. I stopped eating. I stopped drinking. I stopped breathing. I stopped living.

But all this ... this was not my downfall. It was Beirut. She was drowning. I just happened to be in her waters. She, under so much pressure to rebuild overnight, under so much pressure not to cave in to foreign interference, under so much pressure to hold her broken people, she was barely treading above water. Beirut, the city where life and ideas began, was slowly dying. She was turning into plastic. She was becoming cotton candy. She was now pink. She was a dirty needle. She was shit stains on underwear left in the corner of a forgotten room. She was sinking, and like the *Titanic*, she was pulling us all down with her.

At least in war, we had something to fight for. Shopping is boring.

I went to see a doctor. He took one look at me and then prescribed a box of Prozac. How had it come to this? What was happening to Beirut and me? Fear was an abstract person living in my head who constantly reminded me that I was lost. That I could trip over into the abyss at any point in time. That I could become an animal and forget my ethics. One could say that taking pills was the only way for us to stay human. After all, don't we all want to be happy, feel secure, and live? Simply live?

The problems with trying to live in a post-war city are many. Nothing works the way it should. Not even the people. We live under the threat that at any time, things could flare up again. We live under the constant humiliation of the horrible things we did to each other only a few years earlier. I remember the stories of the Holiday Inn. It is one of the highest buildings in Beirut. During the war, it was taken over by a militia who found it entertaining to throw people off the rooftop and try and shoot them in midair. Today we stand side by side as we wait in lines to get into nightclubs.

In post-war Lebanon, large corporations were owned by very few.

The same very few who only a few years ago led their militias onto the streets to kill and rape our city. These men were still reaping the benefits of our lost city, and her people continued to suffer from destitution and shame. These men created a schism in our population; they eradicated the middle class and constructed a modern feudal system. Even now that the war was over, we found that we were still answering to our neighborhood *zaims*; our new lords.

Between us, broken people, a new society was being created. And all the while, we were participating in a collective amnesia.

We constructed an alter reality. With time, it felt as if we had only two choices, to fall into the vortex Beirut was creating or suppress it with a simulated joy. Life in Beirut demanded that you live an altered reality. Some chose pills. Some alcohol. Some heroin. Some denial. At the end of the day, it is all the same thing.

Escapism. Everything was too much to deal with.

Instant gratification. Death was just a door knock away.

Falling. And I was doing it too.

But this could not be happening to me. I became the very person I scorned. And just like everyone else, I blamed Beirut. A Beirut who could not even defend herself.

If I was to avoid the Prozac, I had to come up with a plan. I had to face my reality and take responsibility for my failures. Maybe if I stopped drinking so much. Maybe if I got a job at a bank. Maybe if I wore nail polish and inflated my lips. Maybe if I tried to fit in. You know ...

Just a little bit.

Monsters, be gone!

Growing up, I read a lot of comic books about Superman and Tarzan – those were my favorites. I often wondered if I could be one too?

If I could be a Tarzan? When nothing is as it should be in Beirut, maybe I could be a Tarzan in Beirut.

Maya was over one evening. We were at my parents' house. They were having a dinner party. We snuck a bottle of white wine up to my room and decided to throw our own party. It was winter and the heating was broken. We jumped into my bed, under the blankets, cracked open the bottle and drank it without glasses.

"Maya, I can't keep on like this. I have to get better. It's like, one day, I was convinced that I was going to change Lebanon. I was so strong. I could stand up to anyone. And now look, all I do is drink. I want to forget, but I don't know what I am forgetting."

"Zena, I promise you it will get better soon. Stop being such a drama queen. Why do you hold on to the war so much – you weren't even here! You don't have to solve all of Lebanon's problems yourself. Why are you so guilt ridden? All this ... this has nothing to do with you." She took a large swig of wine, swallowed. "Look, I wish I could make it all go away, but I can't. You have to work with me on this. You cannot start blurring the lines like everyone else. What happened to Beirut did not happen to you. You cannot assume that grief."

"But I feel Beirut ... she is drowning –"

"Zena," Maya interrupted, she wasn't angry, just a little impatient, "one day, we will be in New York together. We'll be old and smelly. We'll take our walks together in Central Park and drink coffee. We'll both have fabulous husbands. And you'll be a famous artist and I'll be a famous writer! Fuck this country, all it does is bring us down." She was always so beautiful when she spoke of New York. Her eyes would glow and a strong but peaceful energy would surround her.

"Maya, the thing is that I only want to be *here*. If only *here* were a better here."

"It's not difficult. You make it difficult. Do you see me caring about what the government is doing or not doing? *Khalas*, enough, if you want to live here, you have to turn a blind eye. You have to not care, just a little. And you have to focus on yourself and not other people's problems. You can't save everyone." Maya turned to hug me. "Dude, I promise you, you will get better. You just have to let go. Let go of the pain. And let go of the drama. And I promise you will see that neither Beirut nor you are sinking. We're all here and we're doing just fine."

"I know. I know what you're saying. I get confused with my reality every now and then. Sometimes when you are crying, I start to cry. I get confused as to who is the one that is really hurt. Sometimes when people ask me if I'm OK, I say no and tell them something that is bothering you. Beirut is like that; we always need drama in our lives. If we don't have it, we appropriate someone else's. We always have to be on high alert and over-caffeinated." She passed the wine to me. It had gone warm. "I can't believe I slept with Haidar in the first place. He was so young. I can't believe I did that," I said.

"I can't believe you did either. It's a miracle you're still in one piece. I really thought that boy was going to break your heart. He almost did."

"He did. That's why I traveled to China last year in the first place. I had to go all the way to the other side of the world to see if I could fix it. I thought that if I could do something worthy that maybe God would mend my heart. I was looking for the lost Druze who are supposed to be waiting behind the Great Wall. I wanted to reunite them with their Arab brothers and sisters. I thought maybe I'd find my husband, because he's obviously not in Lebanon. I thought maybe he was one of the lost Druze in China, like in the folklore. I climbed the wall and looked over. There was no one there. Not a single person. No transmigrated souls. My plan did not work. All I found was plastic."

China flashed before me. The millions of people. The crowds. The future car owners who will eventually surpass the rest of the world in the race to kill our planet. I had my first panic attack when I was there. It lasted for three weeks. For three weeks I was vomiting and crying and passing out and I didn't know why. I thought I was going to die there. I had gone because I wanted to get as far away as possible as I could from Lebanon. China was on the other side of the world – far enough for me. And it was there, when I was all the way on the other side of the world, that I realized that I was a nothing. I was just another face in the crowd. Another consumer. A nothing.

"I thought I was dead," I continued. "I thought I was dead for a long time, but then I came back home. Remember when you picked me up from the airport? You had a bucket with you in case I needed to vomit. I was so happy to see you, I just cried my way out of customs. It was so embarrassing, but I didn't care. I just kept my eyes focused on the bucket."

"You are always crying."

"No. Yes. No. I guess."

"That was a good day, wasn't it?"

"It felt good to come home."

We sat in silence for a few minutes, passing the warm wine between us.

"Why do you think Haidar killed me? Is it because he is Shiite? Someone once told me that Shiite men make the best lovers because they are so passionate."

"It is possible, but I wouldn't know."

"Haidar was so shallow, but he loved me in a way that was new. It was intense and straightforward. But it was also enslaving."

"How so?"

"It was a physical love. He was just so Arabian. Strong, proud and desirable. His nostrils flared when he spoke about music. His dark eyes always had me drunk with love. I was almost afraid to touch him sometimes. When he wore black, I would faint from desire. He was a hallucination of a grand Arabian prince. The ones in the stories that always carried swords and had extravagant and luxuriant mustaches. I would run to him. I would run to him. And run. We were feverishly in love. No ... in lust. I suppose that is all that it was.

"I would ask him to call me Zahra like the girl who was shot by her lover who was a sniper. We used to meet at the empty apartment in the abandoned building, the one with bullet holes from the civil war. It used to smell like cat piss and gunpowder. The building, a faded pink, was covered with posters of political martyrs. The colored glass of the French windows had long since vanished. In the winter it used to be bitterly cold. A damp chill that even the heat of our bodies could not quench. But it would not stop us. In the summer, the heat was oppressive, but we didn't care. Cockroaches roamed free and so did our hearts.

"We drank all the time. We drank wine. We drank whiskey. We drank vodka. We would drink and drink until we were blind with desire. With him, I felt alive because I was always so close to death. In one moment, we could fall. In one moment, I could realize the dream I was living, decide to wake up and ruin everything. But he kept me going until he decided it was over. Until he let me go. Until he let me fall. And crash. And burn.

"He was just like Beirut.

"I used to be so alive. I thought I could have anything I wanted. And then he killed me. One day, he just shot me down, like a sniper."

"You can never possess an illusion," Maya said.

"After we made love for the first time, he told me it was his first time. For a moment, I felt like I did own him. And maybe I did for a while. For a few days at least. Until his body became an addiction and I lost control. But that was a long time ago and I have since paid the price." I sighed. "Maya, despite everything. All this shit. All the disappointments, I'm still very lucky in one way."

"How so?"

I smiled and lay my head on her shoulder, "I have you, dude, I have you." I passed the bottle.

"Please. Don't tell me now you're gay too," she said, shoving the bottle back in my face. "Fuck it, everyone is turning gay."

"Dude! Do I have to be gay to say I love you?" I pounced on top of her and began to tickle her frantically. I was spilling wine on the sheets.

"Stop! OK, I give up." And then she screamed at the top of her lungs, "I love you too!" We were laughing hysterically.

I stood up, bottle of wine still in my hand, and began to jump up and down on the bed around Maya. She could barely breathe as her body was flopping up and down with my jumping. Is it possible to die from laughing too much?

"I love you! I love you! Ooh! Ooh!" I screamed and laughed at the same time. Wine sprayed everywhere. Then my knees buckled and I came crashing down on top of her. "Dude, I got it. I got it."

"What, what, what?"

"If we are to avoid the fatal blue pills, we need to become superheroes."

"Superheroes? OK. Let's do it." Then, after a pause, "but how?"

"I don't know yet. I don't know. But it will come to us soon. Here, drink. We'll figure it out together. Drink. Then let's go and crash the party downstairs. Maybe we can get inspiration from all the layers of make-up and glittery dresses."

Two days and one severe hangover later, I visited my grandmother who lived next to the fishermen's quarters in Ain El Mressieh, one of the oldest neighborhoods of Beirut. She lived in a rooftop apartment overlooking the small wharf. The fishermen, the heart and soul of Beirut, park their tiny blue and white boats every morning, and set sail every night to catch fish. I wondered if this village-within-a-city experienced the civil war like the others.

In my grandmother's house, I came across a small storage room ... a grand door with a small circular vent right in the middle. It was covered with netting, but the netting was covered with dust and dank that must have been at least as old as me. In my grandmother's storage room, I discovered my mother's wedding dress. I had never seen it before. It had a train five meters long. The lace dress was still in perfect condition and I could not resist trying it on. I took off my jeans and laid them gently on top of the table. The dust flew up and I sneezed. More dust flew up and I sneezed again. I remember looking at myself in the mirror. I didn't recognize myself. I guess it was then I realized that I had found my superhero. It was this great and powerful dress. If I wasn't quite ready to face Beirut's brutal realities, I could start slowly behind my mask, deferring the responsibility to the wedding dress. I wondered how far I could take it.

That night, I thought long and hard about my discovery. Sitting in my parents' house, I pulled open the drawer containing the unopened box of Prozac. I gently took it out, gripped it in my hands, and walked out to the balcony. It is almost impossible to stand on a balcony in Beirut and not come face to face with the sea. It is ever present. It stared back at me, violating my wish to be alone. She whispered for me to remember myself. She told me that Beirut was just an illusion.

I opened the box and took out one pill and swallowed it. That was to remind me, always, that I had poison in my body. I put the rest back into the box, and then, let it drop.

It sometimes seems that everything in Beirut is about death and despair, but that is only when she is fooling you. The reality is that she is so full of life that every person wants a part of her. It's a war. It's a gang rape. Constantly.

We ask ourselves why we are still here and how we still survive. But of course this gets us nowhere. Maybe we are the problem and not Beirut? We sit down at cafés on Hamra Street, we sit in cafés by the sea. We drink coffee, we smoke, we smoke, we smoke. Everyone is entitled to their opinions, because technically we live in a democracy. Everyone is affiliated. Everyone is part of a political organization. Or part of an NGO. Or part of a club, or something. We meet, we talk, we smoke, we smoke, and we smoke.

This is our sour poetry of survival.

Much talk with little results eventually becomes abusive to the spirit. I decided that I could not live this life. That if I was going to live in Lebanon, I had to do it my way. I had to be a Tarzan.

One day I went back to my grandmother's house and put the wedding dress on again. It fit perfectly. I had forgotten how wonderful it felt. I left my grandmother's house wearing it, the five-meter train trailing behind me. No one saw me. I jumped into my car and drove away. I decided that I was going to save Lebanon while wearing my mom's dress. I was going to stand up for all the people who had been victimized by their social constraints and held back by their dense and deceitful politicians. I felt good and strong, like I could take on anything. I was definitely not going to get killed today. Not wearing a wedding dress ... it would be too tragic. The "*powers that be*" would never allow it. That stuff only happens in movies. I drove around and around. I drove to places in Beirut that sometimes frighten me. I wanted to see what those areas looked like. I wanted to see and I was not scared because I knew that I was not going to die like this.

In the years since, I wear the dress in times of need. Each time renewing my relationship with Beirut. Each time, rediscovering her.

I walked along the streets and spoke with butchers and bus drivers. I smiled at hysterical women on shopping rampages. I took pity on anorexic girls trying to fit into the latest fashion statements. I sympathized with veiled girls who adorned themselves with fuchsia headscarves, glitter belts, tight white jeans and killer stilettos. When greasy boys on mopeds, with hair stiff with gel, called out sexual insults to me, I waved back and reminded them that their mothers were whores, all with a smile. When mothers came knocking at my door to see if I was ripe and fit for marriage, I bleached my hair a toxic blond. I ate to gain weight. I drank to smell sour. When I got stuck in traffic jams, I pulled out poetry to read. When my friends reached for their anti-depressants, I held their hands. I told them it would soon be over. When men left me, I informed them that I would not be upset, because deep in my heart I knew they would never find anyone like me again. And that perhaps it was a relief for them, because really, I represented a reality they did not wish to acknowledge. I made peace with my family who had always prevented me from becoming a Modigliani, Miller and Basquiat.

I forgave Beirut for wanting to forget, because I understood the burden of humiliation.

11

In order to fully reconcile, you have to dig down to the very core of life in Beirut. You have to be willing to see things for what they really are. You cannot hide behind a magazine sipping coffee on a busy sidewalk. You cannot blind yourself with false ideals. They will all come back to haunt you. You have to walk the streets. You have to talk to her people.

In post-war Beirut, I walk down the streets that hide themselves with fashion boutiques and fast-food diners. I walk down the streets and I see brand new cars parked outside a Starbucks café. I walk to the periphery of the city and I see open sewers. I see balconies with laundry hanging off them. I see tired people who cannot understand why there is so much traffic. I see children walking in the sweltering heat with school bags that must weigh at least 20 pounds. I see children begging for money on the streets. I see silicon lips telling them to "*shoo*" away. I smell stale yogurt. I smell rotting garbage. I walk back into the heart of the city and I see giant cranes giving birth to steel and glass. I see colossal billboards telling me to buy a face cream that will turn my skin from brown to white. I see old men dragging wooden carts behind them trying to sell me vegetables. I see a hair salon that now offers free Botox with every visit. I see teenage girls desperate to become women. I see grown men acting like little boys. I see the sea polluted with oil. I see the scars of the oil spill on our shores. I see the women and children from the refugee camps swimming in this same sea, because they are not allowed to do anything else.

I think the biggest delusion we live with, lies with our government. Our politicians who have blood on their hands. Their armies and warriors now disguised in suits and ties.

The thing with the militiamen is that they never really left. After the civil war, they found themselves jobless. A lot of them went into a sort of depression. They were not allowed to kill, maim, assassinate, rape or pillage any longer. Unexpectedly, they found themselves with so much free time on their hands and no one feared them any longer.

I never really knew about the militiamen until I began clubbing. There was a nightclub we used to go to. It was about forty kilometers north of Beirut. In those days there weren't any nightclubs in Beirut that "decent" girls could go to. You had to visit the Christian part of the country if you wanted to booze up and dance the night away. That was 1994. In those days I drank vodka-orange.

Figaro was a big muscular man and definitely on steroids. He was the bouncer at a popular club called Loco. Figaro was a militiaman during the war, but now he wore black and had his hair slicked back by at least one kilogram of gel. Figaro always wore the same black cowboy boots and silver chain necklace. His shirt, always tight, revealed curly black chest hairs creeping up to this neck. He was, as he described himself, a protector of his street. In Arabic the terminology is *shabeb el sher'aa* which translates to "the youth of the street". He told me that there were many like him. In fact, most men his age, twenty-five, took part in these street gangs.

I liked Figaro because he had kind eyes. And when he told me he had killed people, I refused to believe him. I thought he was just trying to show off, or fit in – one of those things. I used to talk to him about art. I told him about *Guernica*; that people protested war through art. He told me that no one had ever done such a thing for Lebanon. I told him that all artists in Lebanon opposed the war, but the people were too blind to see it. The problem was that people just didn't realize they were looking at art when they were face to face with it. The war had been too crazy. People lost their minds. Their sense of reality. A painting could have been an illusion of reality. A trip. It could take you to places that perhaps you were too scared to go.

"The power of art is beyond us, Figaro," I said as I chugged my orange drink.

"Why don't you like to dance? Why are you always out here bothering me?" he asked. "You know I can't spend all night talking to you."

"Dancing is boring. It is for forgetting. I'm trying to remember."

"But you told me you weren't here during the war. What is it exactly that you are trying to remember?"

"The war started a year before I was born into this present life. I am trying to remember what I was before this bloody war started. All I know now is war, but there must have been a time when I lived the 'golden years.'"

"Your past life? What religion are you?"

"If I told you, you might shoot me. Isn't that what you were doing only two years ago? Why should you be any different now?"

"You are a drunk and stupid girl. Just leave me alone. Anyways, I did not kill people by shooting them. They call me Figaro because I use a shaving knife. A *moos*. Do you even know what that is?"

"Figaro. What do you drink?"

"Whiskey."

"That's disgusting, whiskey tastes like piss."

"After you've killed people, you don't care what you drink as long as you get drunk. Whiskey is good for getting drunk. It doesn't make me paranoid."

"Paranoid? I thought you were tough. Are militiamen allowed to be paranoid?"

"Whiskey," he replied, ignoring me, "is the only way to kill a man, and it is the only way to be able to live with yourself the next day."

I remember giving Figaro a long solemn stare. "May God be with you, Figaro. I need to go back in and dance. I hear my song playing. You should try listening to Dr. Alban."

"Yes, you go back inside. You think you are better than me because you know everything about art and music. But let me tell you something. What you don't know is *life*. The only reason you are standing here today is because of people like me. Without me, this country would be Muslim now, or Israeli or Palestinian. I am the reason that Lebanon exists and you should be grateful."

12

Twelve years have passed since I first moved here and I still find myself trying to make peace with Beirut. Trying to walk her streets to get to know her better. To understand. I often think about running away again. Going back to New York. That four-year break was good in so many ways. But, Beirut, she is selfish with me.

Hamra Street. Once the center of intellectual debate in Beirut, now lined with up-to date fashion stores. The coffee shops that were the center of social revolutions have one by one been replaced with huge multinational clothes stores. The coffee shops I sat in as a student are now filled with lycra and glittery sequence phantasmagoria. There are stores that sell international fashions. Local fashions. And "made in China" fashions. There are cheap-wares, expensive-wares, but mostly there are plastic-wares.

I walk past the stores and feel nauseous. The windows are lined with ultra-thin mannequins. They look at me with painted eyes and try to draw me in to buy their garments. Gold and silver sequined evening dresses tell me to put them on and forget about everything else. To forget about war.

I stare at a mannequin dressed in a purple lycra stretch suit. She tells me that there will always be war, and I have to get used to it.

That at least the latest fashions are still able to come through the Beirut port. That I might as well, at least, look good when I die. That lycra is the best remedy for anxiety. And that turquoise and yellow will make it all go away. That I shouldn't even think of wearing a dress like this before I first get a bikini wax and a French manicure. You have to have the prerequisites. You have to look and feel the part before you can wear the part. That I have to lose at least twenty pounds. That war can be good because anxiety is great for losing weight. All one does is vomit (from fear) and not eat (from lack of food ... and fear).

War is great for the fashion industry.

Please, please, I beg her, there has to be more than this. I know there is. I remember a different time. It wasn't so long ago, but it's getting harder and harder to remember it.

"You are silly," she replied through the glass window, "that was just an illusion. You were in school. It was relative calm. It happens every few years or so. That was not the reality. This is. You cannot base Lebanon on those few years. I have been standing on this street for decades now. Plastic has its benefits. I saw the intellectual debates fall through in the '60s. I saw the activists grow old and create false realities to give themselves the illusion that they had created change. I saw the Israelis drive through in 1982 in their tanks and shoot everything in sight.

"And now I see girls walking around with miniskirts and their bellies pierced. I see veiled women wearing Jimmy Choos under their black blanket. Zena, everyone knows that Beirut is not real. You can create your own reality and live the way you want. It is all a game. There are bigger players who control everything. There is no point trying to change anything because it will not work. Every time the politicians see the Lebanese desperate enough to give up, they inject them with a little bit of vitamins. They will either pass a new law, open a road, or announce new investors. Whatever, it's just to keep you sedated. So really, don't bother. Don't try and change anything. Just live your illusion and don't try to connect with anything outside of Lebanon. This is it. This is life. There is nothing more than here. Any attempt to reach a global dialogue about life, wine, war and everything else will just leave you with disappointments and stress. And you know stress is a major cause of cancer."

I close my eyes and turn away from the mannequin. I don't want her to see me cry. The smell of Starbucks wafts towards me. I bat it away. No internationals for me. No global products. I want my old coffee shop serving bitter shots in tiny fragile white porcelain cups. None of this paper-latte-mocha-grande-crap.

"You know," I am now speaking with my back turned towards her, "I know more about this street than you can ever imagine. I am a participant. You are just an observer. It is my reality, but only your illusion. You may praise your latex shorts and spandex tops and green and gold heels. But you will never be able to know what those fabrics truly feel like on your skin. Latex holds in sweat, giving you a rash. Spandex is artificial and cold, always making your nipples look hard; very unflattering. And green and gold heels arch your back and make you look like an animal in heat."

After that, I find the courage to walk away from the window and continue my journey down Hamra Street. I take refuge in a bookstore, hoping to find my salvation.

I walk to the English section, past all the newspapers with pictures of blown-up body parts, and fashion magazines with pictures of blown-up body parts. I walk down the white wooden stairs. They smell musty. They smell like Beirut. They smell like they have been caught in a time trap of one hundred years. The room is divided into three sections. There are travel books, a small section on religious books, and then everything else. Everything else mostly consists of self-help books and Coelho-esque mystical journeys.

I don't need help, I thought to myself. I just want something good to read. Why is self-help is the only thing that sells in Beirut these days? Is the city really that depressed? Why is everyone looking for a sign to validate their lives? Why does everyone want to read about how there is more than this measly life we live?

At the end of the shelf, I come across a small section entitled Arab writers. I'd never seen it before. Maybe because it was so small. The section on Lebanese writers was even smaller. With disappointment I realized that I had read most of the books already. They were all about the civil war. That war ended fifteen years ago, and we're still writing about it. Will we always only write about war?

I left the bookstore empty-handed and continued my walk down Hamra Street. I got to the end. Now what? I felt that choking sensation that had become so familiar. Beirut trying to strangle me. I pulled a big pink marker from my backpack and drew a big "X" on the wall at the end of the street. The tip of the marker was thick and I dug it in, going over the lines several times. I needed this mark to last forever. I stopped when the tip broke off.

"Beirut. Can you hear me? It ends now. Right here."

That pink "X" at the end of Hamra Street has taken on the role of my guardian angel. A constant reminder that I am alive. And that I am in control. I sometimes forget about it, and then am pleasantly surprised to run into it.

I now see it every time I walk down Hamra.

I see it on my way to my favorite restaurant.

I see it on my way to Maya's house.

I remember seeing it the day I drove to Maya's house and made her wear the super wedding dress. I told her that if she wore it she would not be killed that day. That it would protect her. That it would kill off all her cancer cells. She put it on and got into the car with me. We drove to the Sunday market and she ran around pretending to look for a husband. The day was bright and clear. It was spring. We were having a Beirut spring. In the Sunday market there were men from Syria selling their wares. There were women from Sri Lanka buying the wares that the Syrians were selling. Everything was cheap, everything affordable. Maya ran and ran and men followed and followed. I was waiting in the car. The getaway car. Waiting to scoop her up and make a run for it.

I spotted her coming back through the crowd; she had an entourage. The men were singing and dancing. The women were ululating. Children grabbed her dress for good luck. A chicken was flying somehow over her head. She had a smile a mile long. As she got closer the music grew louder. There were men playing *derbakees* and *nays*. There were women swinging tambourines. There were children singing folk songs. And I couldn't stop laughing. I got out of the car and began to dance around her. I got down on one knee and clapped my hands up at her. We laughed and cried at the same time. Her hair, now red, flew around in waves. Her pearl skin shone like the moon on the sea.

With one jump we were back in the car and sped off into the rest of the day, Maya shrieking with laughter.

"I can't believe I just did that. Why did you make me do that? Why do I always listen to you?"

"What? You never listen to me. Don't try and push this one on me. You practically jumped out of the car as soon as we parked." I reached over and gave her a hug with my free arm. "I told you," now grabbing her shoulders, "a woman never dies in a wedding dress. You are not allowed to take it off ever again."

I wish she'd listened to me.

SUBJECT: love.
To: zena
Fri, 10/29/06 5:11PM 1KB

Jessica told me the v sad news yesterday.

I don't know what to say …

All my love goes out to her family, friends, you and your family.

My brief encounter with Maya was quite unforgettable - because it made me laugh.

I think I've told you this already … but when I asked her what she did in life, she did answer very matter of factly, "I am Zena's best friend". I answered, "fair enough."

Anyways, there are no words really. Wish each and every one of you all the strength.

Much of my love and respect,

k

What they don't tell you about bombs is how loud they are. Your whole house shakes. The windows rattle. The electricity may suddenly go off. You hear your neighbors screaming somewhere down the street. You wish they could just let you sleep. If you slept for one night without any noise or interruptions, perhaps you could handle the stress a little better the next day.

But, you see, they know all this. They know how to stress you out. They do it all on purpose.

In 2006, we played chicken that summer. I refused to leave my city that they were blowing to pieces and they refused to let me sleep. It was a battle to see who could go on longer.

The war ended as suddenly as it began. It is truly astonishing how easy it is to start and end something as complicated as war. After all, it is in the hands of very few people. Very few people have the power to determine the fate and course of your life.

Maya, I lived the war for you. I had to keep you alive. So, I had to keep myself alive first. When they hated, I loved. When they fought to blame, I preached compassion. When they chose sides, I embraced everyone. I knew we were going to make it through. I knew you would live to see the end of it. But you blew me away when you left so soon after. You blew us all away.

I went to your grave and slowly pushed back the white marble slab that was holding you prisoner. I reached in and grabbed for your arm. I knew it was you because I recognized your round spectacular thumbs. The same ones your mom and grandmother have. I pulled you out and you were surprisingly light. You came out with ease. I gently began to unwrap you right there in the graveyard. We were really making a spectacle of ourselves ... as usual. You and me. And Beirut.

In the cab ride back, you told me you were having the strangest dream. That you had left me. It was one of those dreams that seemed so real you actually didn't bother waking up for a long time. I told you that I too had spent most of the rest of October and November asleep, but that after my dream of waking you up, I realized that in order for me to wake up I first had to wake you. You smiled, and through your perfect teeth (minus one small crooked tooth), informed me that's what friends were for.

We left the graveyard so relieved. I knew you could not be dead. It was still too soon. It wasn't your time to go.

Beirut loomed ahead of us in all her glory. I was anxious and not ready to jump back in. It was somehow nice out here in the pine tree suburb. So quiet. Even the great public park surrounding the graveyard with its mighty pines was empty. It was closed during the civil war and had not yet reopened. These days, pine trees are only for dead people.

Our journey was to the land of the living.

One would say it was odd to think of Beirut as living. Beirut is a dusty concrete jungle and concrete is far from being alive. But she is. She is magnificent. Beirut constantly reminds me of what it's like to lose what you love most in the world. She gives and gives and then she takes it all away. You have to be alive to be able to pull that off.

Maya, when I came back for you in the cemetery, do you remember our conversation?

"I'm so glad you found me," you said.

"Me too," I replied.

"How did you know which one I was in? There are like a million graves here."

"I opened the one that had the sunflowers on it."

"But didn't you put them there?"

"Yes, I did."

"How did we ever get here?"

"I don't know, it was a bad dream, I guess."

"I'm so glad you found me. I was starting to give up."

"It took so long because you were actually away for a while. You went up to heaven and had to face God. Then you were sent back down to battle some demons in your grave. I was worried you may not know what to say to them. I didn't know if you knew religious texts in Arabic or not. I had to wait until it was over before I could get you."

"I remember now. Yeah, I didn't know what to say, but the words just came out by themselves. I think someone was helping me."

"I got so worried and tired of waiting so I read out the texts above your grave for you. I guess you heard."

"I guess I did. Thanks."

"No worries."

"Can we go home now?"

"Yes. Let's."

I went to your grave and I lay down next you. I asked which way your head was facing and they told me and so I adjusted myself. I lay down next to you like I've done so many times before. I told you how much I missed you. And that it was time to come home now. There wasn't much space between your grave and the next one. The dirt ground between the marble slabs was damp from last night's rainfall. I lay my cheek on the cool earth and called your name. You heard me right away. I was surprised. I thought it would take longer. With my right hand I pushed at the heavy marble slab. It didn't budge. I readjusted my body and used my right leg too. My back was pressed up against the grave behind me. I apologize now for trespassing.

The slab moved a little and I squeezed my hand inside. I could only feel darkness. The hole was deeper than I imagined. I was groping at nothing. I called out your name and asked for help. I felt four arms reach out. My hand brushed against them one by one until I found yours. I recognized you by your thumbs. Those big round thumbs that always made you drop things. I used to count how many things you would drop in a day. Number one. Number two.

I held on to your hand and pulled and pulled. I squeezed you out of the dark crack in the marble. You came out like jelly and slowly reassembled yourself. I sat up, brushed the dirt off my cheek and cradled you in my arms. Like Michelangelo and Madonna. I ran my fingers over your lips and the tiny freckle under your eye.

"I was waiting for you."

"I know. I'm so sorry I took so long."

"Where were you?"

"I was stuck at home. There was a war going on. It lasted thirty-four days. That is why it took so long."

"Couldn't you have come during the war?"

"No. They were blowing up everything around the graveyard. It was too dangerous. I'm so sorry you had to wait so long. We had no idea when it was going to end."

"Wow. Are you OK?"

"I'm not so sure. They hit all the roads and bridges. They hit fuel and food supplies. It was really scary. It was so loud. I had never heard bombs exploding before. They were being dropped from planes. And the planes were so loud too. Sometimes there were planes without people in them that would fly around all night, but we could not see them. They sounded like mosquitoes. I kept wanting to smack them with a swatter, but I could not reach them. They made me think of my brother who smacks mosquitoes against his wall and leaves them there as a lesson for other mosquitoes who dare to trespass. I wondered if he was thinking of smacking the planes while he was huddled up in his room without electricity and internet. Would he use his bare hand as usual?

"So many people were killed. I had so much trouble finding your grave. This place got so much bigger all of a sudden."

"I heard a lot of noise. Zena, this seems very familiar. Are you sure I wasn't still alive when this happened? I can't remember anything anymore. Everything seems so hazy. It's as if there has always been war. One war after the other. Which one exactly are you talking about? What did they do?"

"They dropped bombs all over Beirut. Entire neighborhoods disappeared. Entire families gone. They used bombs that were so powerful, they could burn through concrete buildings. They called them bunker buster bombs. I imagined that each bomb had a sort of fist attached to it. That the fist would fall first smashing the buildings in half and then the bomb would explode. Like in the *Tom and Jerry* cartoons. The old ones that look like they were made during World War II. They also dropped bombs that burnt people. Their skin melted right off. And, they dropped bombs that had hundreds of little bombs in them for little kids to pick up and explode. They didn't discriminate. Everyone was allowed to pick up a bomb.

"I am glad you were dead because I didn't want you to experience it. It was really horrible. Worse than all the stories we ever heard about. They kept throwing bombs and no one stopped them."

"Zena, I was technically still alive. Barely. But the morphine I was taking for my pain sent me somewhere else. I remember now. They say that once a cancer patient starts with the morphine, there is no turning back. I'm sorry I wasn't there for you. I'm sorry you had to go through it alone."

"They are saying there is supposed to be another one next year. How is it that they plan these things? Has it really become so easy?"

"I don't know."

"Maybe it's better if you go back down. I can come with you this time."

"You think?"

"We can just hide out until it's over. Or until the world ends. Either way, at least we'll be together again."

"Only if you really want to. It kind of sucks down there. Everyone speaks Arabic and I don't understand much. Plus, they don't have microwave popcorn."

"I think I'll take my chances. Move over."

I moved you over to a tree for some shelter. I was worried people would think it strange talking to you. I told you about the Beirut you missed out on while you were gone. About how so many people have come to her. About how so many have wooed her with their promises and proclamations. So many have used her, drooling madness into her ears. About how she has become every person's whore. But we've always known that, haven't we?

You said that you had missed everyone while you were away, so I told you some stories.

I told you about how my brother, Nadim, had finally come to terms with Beirut through his theory of the *Maganatise*. I told you about how Nadim believes that the reason people are so aggressive in Lebanon is because the electro-magnetic waves emanating from the ground under Beirut are too strong. They create a lot of energy that makes people angry, frustrated and down-right mean. I told you that on a bad day, my brother can often be quoted saying, "the *Maganatise* is strong today."

You laughed out loud. And I almost started crying. I realized then how much I had missed you.

"Would you like to know what I really think?" I asked you. And before you could ask me to continue I stood up and placed my closed fists in front of my face and spoke directly to them, like Bruce Lee reciting an important history.

"My counter theory is that it is not the *Magnatise* that is upsetting everybody, but rather the souls of the dead roaming the streets of Beirut. People who were killed by snipers, bombs, explosions, assassinations, and mines. Most of these people died for no reason, didn't receive proper funerals, and now they are really upset and are taking it out on the living. The worst spots are the tunnels. People were killed there in hundreds and their bodies left to rot for ages. I'd be pretty pissed off too. I try and avoid the tunnels as much as I can. I don't blame you for having never wanted to drive."

At this point, a sober darkness swept over your face. You looked down at your hands. They were spread open on your lap, palms facing down. You were sitting propped up against the tree. Your skin was whiter than the burial cloth they had wrapped you in, that had now unraveled itself from your body and lay jumbled at your side. Your hair was long again. It was red as the fire you had always hoped it could be. It fell over your shoulders and hid your breasts. I brought my fists down slowly, turning my head away as a blush crept over my face. You are as beautiful as I had always imagined you to be. Why could I never tell you before?

"Is that what happened to me?"

"No. You actually survived the war. It was your broken heart that killed you a few days later."

"Tell me a better story. Did you paint while I was away?"

I wanted to tell you that I did. But I was too embarrassed to lie.

"I couldn't make art during the war. It was too difficult. I wanted to. I wanted to make something so great that it could change the world. But I couldn't. My head was tight all the time and I kept feeling like I was going to vomit. I didn't know if it was stress or a disease. They were dropping all kinds of things on us. Maybe it was both."

"I'm sorry you had this block."

"No, it wasn't a block. It was more than that. It was absolute despair. How could I be painting when people all around me were dying? I couldn't paint death. I didn't want to paint death. I didn't want to give the war any more importance than it was already imposing on me. If I painted the war, I would be giving in. I would have somehow accepted that I could live through a war in some semi-normalcy. I would have proved that war could be acceptable. I was almost afraid of what it could produce in me. What if the painting was good? What if it was the greatest thing I ever made?"

I think I finally understood what Tim was trying to say to me in New York.

"What is better? To live in absolute chaos or to be caught up in the New World order? A system in which pure emotions are replaced by French fries and cheese. Where love becomes anonymous sex and people have forgotten how to cry. Where people laugh on cue. A system where every other person dies of an incurable cancer?"

"Isn't there something in between?"

"I don't know." You paused for a few moments and then looked up at me. It was dark now. "Are you not afraid of being here in the dark?"

"I didn't realize the sun had set already. I guess I am afraid. Or at least, I could be if I start to think about it."

You then asked me to come and sit next to you. At first I was grateful, because I knew you would make me feel safe. But then, I realized that you were still unclothed and a wave of embarrassment came over me.

"Are you not cold?" I asked, extending my scarf over to you.

"No. Not really. Can you believe it's already November and I don't feel cold. I can't feel a thing. Maybe it's this climate change thing."

I bent my knees and plopped down beside you. I wrapped you up in my scarf. I had been meaning to ask you a question all day and figured that it was OK to ask now. I took your hand in mine and ran my index finger over your thumb.

"Did you see me when you left? By your hospital bed, I wore pink so that you could see me when you left. I knew you were going that day. I tried not to cry because I wanted you to be happy when you left. I wanted to be strong for you. So you wouldn't get worried about me … about us."

Your eyes opened wide and you stretched your arm across and pulled me close to you.

"Of course I did."

I started to cry. Like a mother who had lost her child, I heaved. I cried for you. I cried for me. I cried for Beirut.

Finally.

The moon was at midnight now. I was crouched under the mulberry tree. The air was crisp. A comforting pale light reflected off the trees.

I drank in the beauty of the moment. I was so grateful just to be able to be with you again. I didn't want it to end. I wanted to pour my heart out to you. I wanted to tell you all the things I couldn't before. But instead, I found that I was now staring out into your disappearance. I stood up and frantically began calling out your name. I ran back to your grave, but you were not there. I ran around the whole cemetery pulling my hair out and screaming your name. I called and called for you, but you had gone.

The moon had vanished and I was enveloped by a complete darkness. I flung myself on top of the marble slab covering your grave. The same one that contains your aunt, your grandmother and your grandfather. I rolled on to my back and stretched my arms out to the sinister sky. I couldn't believe I had lost you again.

I wanted to tell you things.

That while you were dead Beirut had also died with you.

One night, they bombed our electricity plants and there was no light in the city. So, I drove to the sea. I followed the tiny gas lights from the fishermen boats and they lead me down to the Corniche. I got out of the car and walked towards the sea. I wanted to be as close as I could. It was calm and quiet and almost deceased. It was so dark that I could not see the horizon. The sea and the horizon were one. I was afraid. It was as if I had walked off the Earth. But it was also extremely breathtaking. That obscurity somehow filled me with love. I thought about our neighbors who did this. Our neighbors, who dropped bombs on our electricity plants. And in some ways I wanted to thank them. Because they put my city on hold, long enough for me to take a break and walk down to the sea. The war gave me all the time I needed to think.

I thought about my life. About my family and friends. I thought about what I may do tomorrow. About if I was going to have children or not. The wind had picked up and it was blowing through my hair. I felt beautiful. And tears crawled down my face. Why was I always crying?

So typical, I thought to myself. Arab women always have something to cry about. And as much as I try and deny it, it is in my blood.

"Don't resist," the sea murmured to me.

I turned my back to the sea and felt her foam spray on my neck. I looked at Beirut with hungry eyes. I could not find her. There were no cars. No people. No light. My car began to disappear. I closed my eyes, feeling a panic come over me. Counted to ten backwards. It was no use. Tried it again in English. I began to tremble. And then there it was ... in a flash, time squeezed itself in two. I felt a great pressure surge through my body. A crack of thunder filled my head. My throat felt like it was going to explode. My ears like they were vomiting blood. Beirut detonated right before my eyes and I was going out with it. I grabbed on to the blue railing that separated me from the water.

I closed my eyes and a white light flooded my vision. I cupped my hands over my ears and bent down as if to duck an illusionary projectile. Images poured through my head. I saw Parisians in Paris sipping *café au lait*. I saw New Yorkers in New York fighting their way down Fifth Avenue. I saw Lagosians in Lagos clinging on to yellow, tilted, overfilled buses. I saw subways moving at light speed and jets crossing the universe. I saw puppies waiting to be adopted. I saw a young bride losing her virginity. I saw a young girl losing her clitoris. I saw someone flipping hamburgers. I saw someone holding a gun. And as soon as all this began, it all ended.

Everything was still as it was. The darkness had resumed. It had just been a sonic boom. Just another one of our neighbor's jets flying into our airspace. Just another one of those jets that break the sound barrier. And break my heart.

My heart.

"Don't resist," the sea whispered to me. I didn't this time. I fell to the ground and cried and cried and screamed. I screamed into the darkness, asking how long did I have to continue living in fear like this? How long were we, Beirut and I, going to continue to be raped like this?

14

I woke up this morning not to find Mazen at my side.

I turned over and the bed seemed to stretch for endless miles. The white sheets carried faint stains of periods and dog saliva. I called out his name, but the response I got back was the chilly echo of purple cinderblock walls.

Turning a blind eye to the clock next to my table, I rolled over onto my side and wondered if there was going to be electricity or water today. I had to wash my sheets. I wanted to take a shower with hot water. I wanted to water my plants. I wanted to watch some news on TV. I needed to send some emails.

It was hot. The windows were shut. To keep the noise out.

I picked up my cell phone; I only had two bars of power left. It had not charged during the night. There had been no electricity. I wanted to call Mazen to see where he was. How could he slip out without me hearing him? These days we were sleeping very little because of the bombs. I guess he left when I finally fell asleep.

I got out of bed, slowly. My back was hurting me, again. I turned around to see that Tapi, my dog, was curled up next to me. The bombs scared her. She began sleeping in our bed when the war started.

"Tapi, you silly dog. Every morning, it's the same thing. If you're going to share this bed with us, you can't be a bed hog! Look, I'm almost off the bed. You can't keep pushing me around like this." She looked up at me with her tender eyes, stretched her back and yawned. "Tapi, I'm serious. I need my sleep and I can't have my back hurting every morning I wake up. I have to be alert. I have to be functional. We are at war."

I made my way out of the bedroom and inspected the house. Did anything happen while I was asleep? Maybe Mazen was in another room. I fiddled with the light switch. No electricity. I walked into the kitchen. I realized that I would have to find a way to go shopping today. We were down to two bottles of water, some pasta, and a crate of beer.

"Mazen," I called out.

No answer.

"Mazen ..."

Silence.

I looked down at Tapi, "Where do you think he is?"

No answer.

I walked out to the balcony, the sun glared at me. It was hot. Stifling, almost. What time was it anyway? My plants had begun to wilt. It was inevitable, they were innocent victims. There are always innocent victims during war. I walked back to the kitchen, grabbed the water and poured a few splashes into Tapi's bowl. Then I went back to the balcony and gave a few drops to my favorite basil plant. Yes, I had a favorite, and I vowed that it would survive this war with me. I went back into the bedroom and picked up my cell phone.

Fuck it. I called Mazen on speed dial. "Where are you, quick, low battery."

"*Hayeti*, my love, I didn't want to wake you, but my father called.

He was having a panic attack. He thinks we should leave Ashrafiyeh because there could be a civil war again. He was worried the Christians would kill us."

I started laughing. "Is this what happens in war? People lose their minds and their ability to rationalize situations. Did you remind him that we are under attack from another country this time?"

"*Hayeti*, don't be like this. You know how it is with old people. I am just going to stay with them for a while until they calm down. Apparently the bombs were really loud last night here on this side of town. They're just a little shaken up. See you later? Kiss Tapi for me. Love you, bye."

I crawled back into bed. Tapi followed. I just didn't have the energy to get through another day of this. I thought about Mazen's parents. Even now, we still refer to Beirut as East and West. Though the civil war that once divided the city had been over for more than fifteen years, we could not shake the habit of believing that each religion should stick to their side of town. Even though I do not belong to the religion that this side of town is supposed to protect, I feel safe and warm in my bed. Home is where the heart is.

Mazen and I had been married for two years now. When we got married, we decided to live in Ashrafiyeh specifically to prove a point. That Lebanese should once again live as one people, and not be divided by religion. We were so in love, believing that our love could change the world. I hugged Tapi close to me.

Strewn glasses of wine lay upturned by the foot of my bed. There were two. I stopped drinking when the war started, but last night, I couldn't take being sober any longer. It was so difficult to fall asleep so I drugged myself with wine. I just needed to sleep. Just at least for one night. The paranoia that had begun to settle in was only due to sleep deprivation. After a while, with war, some things become repetitive enough that you can forget what life was like before.

It had become a pattern. The Israeli army is good with patterns. They are mechanical and precise like clockwork. They bombed us every night. They bombed the south of the city. They bombed bridges and highways. Last night they hit the airport again. I wondered if there is anything left there to hit. We were short on fuel now with the barricade at sea. They weren't allowing any fuel into the country. Cars lined up at gas stations all day, just to get a few drops into their tanks. There wasn't enough to go around. How is it physically possible to turn a country upside down, overnight?

I am so naïve when it comes to the marvels of modern-day technology.

Does this mean I can't drive around Beirut anymore? Can't see my friends? Am I doomed to ride this war out alone? My days I can handle, but what is to happen to me at night when they start to bomb again? When I run out of candles? When I can't pretend to ignore the deafening explosions anymore? I don't want to die alone.

I thought about Mazen. His heart, so big. Always wanting to take care of everyone, but himself. Last night he told me he loved me. It was hot. As hot as a sticky summer Beirut night could be. The jasmine bush under our balcony was in full bloom. Its scent was heavy and dreamy, almost as demure as Angelina Jolie's lips. Everything was perfect. The smell of his coffee skin. His dark hair and honey eyes. The full moon. The jasmine. And the bombs. "I love you, my love," his breath tickled my ear.

Is it right to make love when others are dying.

Is it right to make love when children are being killed by bombs. By phosphorous bombs that burn off their skin. By phosphorous bombs that, if you lived to survive them, leave their mark on you forever.

People wonder why I don't have any children. I am thirty years old and here in the open sore that is the Middle East, people think that I am either insane, sterile or have marital problems because I don't have children.

I don't have children because I am afraid to have children. I am afraid of dying and leaving them here alone. I am afraid of global warming swallowing them up. I am afraid of yet more war and disaster. Yes, they could be blown to smithereens by an Israeli jet invading our airspace. Yes, "Big J" could be re-commissioned. They could contract Ebola, West Nile Virus, Malaria or Whooping Cough. All these things could happen and more.

After I realized that there was going to be no electricity, no water and no fuel, I went out to look for a bicycle. I walked for a few kilometers in the direction of Ashrafiyeh's city center. The streets were empty. Wooden window shutters mostly closed. A good number of my neighbors had evacuated the city, taking shelter in their mountain homes. It felt surreal. Another long Hollywood movie. I thought about that scene in the Stephen King book, when all the people on Earth die, except for a handful. I remembered how they walked into stores and took anything they wanted. Cool. But this was Beirut and the reality of empty streets was horrible. In Beirut, evacuations happen all the time. People padlock their stores knowing they will eventually come back. Looting would not be a good idea.

I got to the center and found a few stores open. It was a sigh of relief to see the bike store open too. I would have been so disappointed if I had walked all this way for nothing. Apparently, I was not the only one with the brilliant idea. There were two other people in the store.

"Hi Ramzi," I said, waving to the store owner when I walked in. "I guess it's a good season for you. War." He wasn't sure if I had thrown him a joke or an insult. I felt embarrassed. "Sorry, what I meant was that, with no more fuel in the country, people have realized the advantages of biking. Hey, at least we'll have a clean city now."

"You shouldn't buy a bicycle just because there is war. It is eventually going to end. I hope you're not going to spend all this money on something you will only use for a week or two," Ramzi replied pragmatically.

"Oh, no, no, I've been meaning to get into shape. Well, now's as good of a time as any other." What was I doing, lying to Ramzi like this. He is the only Lebanese to have climbed Mount Everest. In fact, he was supposed to be leaving Beirut in a month to climb K2, the last mountain of his seven-summit challenge. How could I be lying to a man like this? I walked through the store looking at the bicycles. They were all so hi-tech. I felt too embarrassed to ask for help. I found myself at the back of the store looking up at a big color photograph. It was a man in a red parka with a black mask over his face holding up the Lebanese flag.

"Ramzi, is this you on Everest?"

"Yup. I couldn't take the mask off. It would have been too dangerous. Some things are not worth the risk. The challenge was to climb the mountain, not to gain fame with a picture of my face."

"Yes, you are right. What a wonderful moment it must have been."

"It was, but I also understood that it was simply a brilliant moment of many more to come. Life is what you make of it. This war, this is nothing. It will come and go. You have to keep focused on the goal. You cannot let external things direct you. If I did, I would have never made it up the mountain. There were so many unexpected challenges. But I stayed focused, believing that I was going to get to the top. Everything else was a distraction not worth my time."

"You are right. I wish I was as strong as you."

Ramzi chuckled to himself, "I just hope we have an airport again so I can fly out. Anyways, if we don't I'll just hike over to Syria and catch a plane from there. Nothing is going to stop me from finishing my challenge."

After Ramzi's impressive speech, I realized that my will to bike had left me. They were all too complicated, with too many gears. How was I ever going to get through this war if I could not even manage to choose a bicycle? Why did things have to get so complicated?

I took my phone out of my pocket. Still on two bars. I decided to risk it and call my brother Nemo. I asked him to meet me at the store.

"What? You want me to come all the way out there? Are you crazy? I'm not wasting my fuel on this."

"Nemo, please, I really need help. It's such a simple thing, and I feel that if I don't do it, I will crack. Please you have to understand, it's just something I need to do. I just have to get one thing done today. Please?"

"OK, hang up. Don't waste your battery on this. I will see if I can find a cab. I'll only come if I find a cab. Wait twenty minutes. If I don't show up, go home and forget about the bike."

Exactly twenty minutes later, Nadim showed up in a battered cab. He was arguing with the cab driver who was apparently trying to extort him for money.

"Ten dollars is more than enough. You know this ride should only cost three!"

"It's war, I have to feed my family. And you made me drive into East Beirut. Haven't you heard? There is talk of civil war!"

"Are you crazy? It's the Israelis who are attacking us. Here is twenty, now drive away." And the cab driver did.

"Hey Ramzi, hi Zee!" Nadim strutted in feeling proud of himself. He had expected to pay around fifty dollars for the cab ride. "For thirty bucks, what kind of a bicycle can I buy for my sister?"

We all laughed and Ramzi took us around the store. Everything looked so complicated. There were so many gears and chains. What happened to the days when you picked your bicycle based only on color? Where had all the pink bikes gone? I gave up, but Nadim ended up purchasing a bike of his own. One with a lot of gears and chains. He thought that biking under the bombs was a brilliant idea. We left the store happy. My brother beaming at his new bicycle, myself, happy at the comical vision of him dodging bombs on his bicycle.

I hopped on the back, and he rode standing up. We rode through the streets of Beirut and I felt like I was in an old Italian black and white flick. My hair was blowing in the wind ... the few people who dared to be out pointed at us and laughed ... it was good for a while. I forgot about the war. I remembered that this was the Beirut I knew and loved so much. It felt good to love Beirut again. I just wanted to enjoy the moment. I put the bombs out of my head. At least for one afternoon.

I looked up at my brother pedaling away. His bald spot at the crown of his head was beginning to show. He looked so much like dad now. I was overcome by a sweet sadness. I was nostalgic for our childhood. He was pumping away, taking me further from my side of Beirut, but I felt safe and protected. Like an eagle, he was swooping down to save me and bring me home to my family. I smelled his sweat trickling down his back and wondered if I smelled the same too. Do families have the same smell? We are only eleven months apart in age. I wondered if our livers and kidneys look alike. I wondered how similar we were on the inside.

I could hear his heart beating so strongly as he struggled with my weight behind him. I could see his eyes squinting trying to avoid the glare of the Mediterranean sun. I was so happy I wanted to cry. I had forgotten how beautiful it could be to feel warmth. As his weight shifted from side to side, I closed my eyes to the rhythm of his movements and began to remember our childhood in Africa, where we used to ride like this all the time. I remembered how we used to go out in the torrential rain and ride through the dirt roads that became rivers. We used to see who could outride the other, trying to push through the water current that was building up.

The sewers on the sides of the road would fill up and it would become impossible to tell them apart from the road. We used to play chicken and see who could pedal farthest before falling into the open sewers.

"Zena, look, more people are leaving." Nadim stopped the bike. We were on the Corniche now.

I got off the bike and leaned against the blue metal railing. I opened my eyes towards the Mediterranean. Three ships stood in the harbor. One was a giant white cruise ship, the other two were gray battleships. I could barely make out French flags at their masts. The ships were being boarded by Lebanese who did not want to ride out the war. They were not willing to see the outcome. They did not have faith in their country. They had been betrayed before.

"Nemo, I think we're the only ones left here. Maybe we should go too. We weren't here during the civil war, we don't know the reality of war. Maybe we're making the wrong decision to stay. We have no idea what it was really like. What if it goes on forever? What if we want to leave one day, but find out that there are no more boats left to take us?"

"I really don't know ... but I thought you wanted to stay anyways."

"I do. I don't know why, but I do. I feel like if I leave now, I will never be able to come back. And that idea scares me more than death. Anyways, Tapi isn't allowed on the ships and I'm not leaving her behind. Maya is sick, she needs me. I need her. Mom will never leave. Lana will never leave."

"You would risk your life for your dog."

"My dog. My best friend. My family. All of them, yes. Yes, I guess so. Nemo, look at us. I mean really look at us. Look at this sea. What else is there? This is our life. Our reality. We are not New Yorkers working in 100-floor buildings. We are not Chinese people becoming economically empowered. We are Lebanese caught in a time trap. There was always war. There will always be war. It has always been like this. The Romans sailed in and out of this harbor. Alexander came. Hannibal came. Napoleon. Rumsfeld and Rice. They are all the same. We are in a delicate position and it is our fate to be doomed. We just have to get used to it. Everyone wants a piece of Lebanon, and Lebanese want to be like everyone else – we are stuck."

"Whatever. I'm hungry. Let's go home."

When we got home, stinky and sweaty, I rushed to hug my parents. I didn't realize how much I had missed them.

"Zena, why can't you stay with us until this stupid stupid war is over?" Mom's eyes looked tired. Sophia Loren had been betrayed. God forgive us.

I wanted to say yes, yes, yes. I didn't want Mom to be in this position. She deserves Capri Island and dark Chanel sunglasses.

She deserves the simple things in life with the possibility of a free upgrade. A glorious sunrise over honeydew melons and a warm tickle of wind in her hair as she looks over to Dad with loving eyes and a fertile womb.

But instead, I said, "Mom, we cannot live in fear. Who knows when this war will be over with. Don't worry; I am fine where I am. We cannot hide. We cannot show them that we are afraid." I knew that she believed in all that I was saying because she was not willing to leave either. She just wanted me in her arms.

I wanted to hide in her hug and stay there forever. But my stupid pride, always in the way, made me want to look strong. I wanted to show her that if she could live through a war thirty years ago, I could too. So silly. So unbelievably stupid.

Nadim put his arm around Mom's shoulder, "Don't worry, Mom, when you miss her, I'll just go and get her with my bike again. See, we don't need fuel or anything now. And the Israelis can't detect me moving on the bike, so we are safe too."

My brother is the funniest person I know. A long time ago, just before I moved to Beirut, he had a talk with me. He told me not to let it get to my head. Not to go crazy.

"You know what these Beirut people are like. They're all crazy because of the war. The war is not the only thing that will make you crazy. It's also the family. Family is really tight there. It's too much. Aunts and cousins and uncles and grandparents and friends of the family and family that live up in the mountains and family that live in Syria. Zena, they will make you crazy, promise me you will not become crazy too."

I promised him that I would retain my mind. That I would never let myself get comfortable enough with the idea of war. Comfortable enough with the idea, because you turn a blind eye if you want to survive years and years of bloodshed and destruction. You have to still be able to go out and buy your vegetables even though there is a possibility that your car could get blown up. You still have to be able to go and visit friends, maintain some sort of a decent social life, otherwise you will find yourself talking to your cinderblock walls. You have to be able to go out for a coffee or a drink, and convince yourself that you couldn't possibly live without an episode of *Sex and the City*, because if you do, you may just crash and burn. With the whole world moving ahead, you don't want to be left behind. When people outside have moved from styrofoam to paper, you want to be able to do the same. When pastels are no longer in on TV, you want to throw yours out.

When you notice no one wears shoulder pads anymore, you cut up your old tops. When men on TV are becoming more and more like women, you want your husband to follow the trend; be a stay-at-home dad, crack jokes about his weight and housework, and then kick back a few beers with his buddies at the end of the day, all the while being able to fit into a beautiful Tom Ford Gucci velvet jacket.

That night my mom cooked a big feast. We sat down at the dining-room table. We were all there, surrounded by a huge feast. We drank wine. We ignored the bombs. We understood that if we were going to die, at least we were together, and our bellies would be full. I felt like I was in one of those World War II movies; a rich Jewish family sits down to dinner, not willing to believe what is happening around them, and then suddenly the Gestapo walk in and start shooting. I saw the crystal glasses shatter, I saw my sister grab the dogs and hide under the table, I saw my father shot down, red blood on his white linen shirt, my mother screaming hysterically. I saw my brothers jump up and try and wrestle the gunmen down.

I blinked my eyes and tried to push the thought away. I wanted to be happy for my parents tonight. I didn't want them to worry about me. We hadn't had a meal like this together in a long time. I tried to memorize every detail of the night because I thought that one day I might have to recreate this security for my own children.

There will be war again, my children will experience it, whether I like it or not. It is a Lebanese reality.

15

We are tired.

It has been almost a year since our summer war ended; however, the bombs are still present. This time they are from our own backyard. Politicians and journalists are being assassinated, and the whole country is divided over the conclusion of who's behind it all. The country is literally split in half and there are fears of a new civil war erupting.

Those assassinated: politicians (and their bodyguards who happened to be in close vicinity), journalists, innocent bystanders or civilians in the wrong place at the wrong time

The method: car bombs.

The perpetrators: unknown.

Conclusion: we're all fucked.

When the first few car bombs went off, I found myself very blasé about it.

The very first one went off at the other end of my neighborhood. We were at home, having take-out sushi, when I heard a large boom followed by rattling windows.

"It's a bomb, isn't it?" I turned to Mazen, no fear in my eyes. I was surprised. It had been months since I heard anything like it, months since the never-ending summer war ended, but I still recognized the sound.

"No, no, don't worry, it's just fireworks."

"Mazen, it's OK, you don't have to lie to me. If I survived the last war, I can do this one. We have no choice, right? Just please don't lie. I realized last summer that if I want to live here, I have to be prepared for the reality of life here. I am a different person now. I don't care about anything anymore. I am not afraid of dying." It was true, since Maya left, everything had changed. I am not afraid of dying. I now understand that I will eventually die. So will my husband. And my family. And Mom. And Dad. Tapi. My children. This is life.

Life without Maya. It feels like even during war, life seemed to be a little better. Because there was Maya.

I remember one day, half-way into the summer war, Maya and I decided to break the norm, leave the house and head for the beach. We needed to get out of the house for a bit. By then, we'd realized there was a pattern to the Israeli bombing. Within the idiocy of war, there was a small reliable system that emerged: 3:00 PM until 6:00 PM. That's when they took a break.

"We just have to make sure we get home before it starts to get dark, because that's when they usually start bombing Dahiyeh," Maya claimed. "Fuck it, I'm not letting my whole summer go to waste. Like radiotherapy isn't stressful enough – if the summer passes by without us going to the beach at least once, I'll join Hezbollah and start fighting back."

We thought the safest place to go would be the Movenpick Hotel by the infamous Pigeon Rocks. It was where all the journalists were staying and broadcasting their reports. There wasn't much of a beach, but we were happy to hit the pool. Our only fear was that with the tight security, there was a big chance that we would not be allowed in.

At 3:00 PM exactly, I left my home and headed towards Maya. She was waiting for me under the awning of her building. Her headscarf tied haphazardly around her head. She looked a little worried, but it was understandable. Maya, young and divorced, with scars on her lower back from the radiology, bald from the chemotherapy, had every right to be a little worried about taking time out to hit the beach in the middle of a war.

"*Yalla*, let's do this, sucker." Her Mr. T accent filled my car, as she jumped in and gave me a hug.

"Yeah! Let's go find you a hottie foreign journalist too."

Maya turned and smiled. "You want to see something totally cool?" She pressed down the button to automate the sliding roof of my convertible Smart car. After the roof opened up all the way, she jumped on top of her seat, stood through the roof and yanked her headscarf off. "Tada! Look Beirut, look at me now."

I, driving as fast as possible, turned my head to look at her. Through the roof and the glare of the summer sun, I saw that Maya had on a light blue rubber swim cap. It was adorned with daisies. Something I had given to her nearly ten years ago. I couldn't believe she still had it.

"No one has to see my fucking bald head." she screamed at Beirut. She plopped down on her seat and her eyes were teary. I wasn't sure if she was crying, or maybe it was just the wind in her eyes. I didn't ask.

We made it to the hotel in one piece and miraculously were granted entry into the pool. I think the security guard assumed we were prostitutes called in by the hotel for one of their guests.

Maya, unashamed of her scars, ripped off her pants and dove

straight into the pool. I barely threw off my sandals and followed her in. It was heaven. We floated on our backs for a while without saying anything. It was good. The silence was good. After a few minutes, the wind pushed our bodies closer together. I felt her elbow brush against my waist. I reached out for her hand, gently, so neither one of us would flip over.

"Maya, dude, you realize that you could have anyone here that you wanted? Foreigners love divorced Lebanese women. Like, they know that you've already been deflowered, so that automatically turns them on to you because they assume that you will go all the way with them." She giggled quietly and we just kept floating. This was the first time we had done anything fun since she began her chemotherapy.

We continued to float.

That was a year ago.

Now, there is a new war. In one month, six bombs went off in different parts of town. Another pattern has developed. A bomb goes off. You somehow hear about it. You either actually hear it, or someone calls you to make sure you are OK. With the last one, the way I found out was through a friend of mine in Yemen. He sent me a text message on my phone. I ran to the TV and there it was: an explosion right next to my parents' house. I had no idea. I had been out on my balcony watering my plants for the past half hour. I didn't hear it. The wind was blowing away from me that day.

When a bomb goes off in Beirut, the first reaction is to pick up the phone and call all your loved ones and make sure they are OK. Then you call their parents. Then you call any friends who may live in the area the bomb went off in. Because everyone who owns a phone is calling at the same time, it is usually difficult, technically, to connect and emotionally straining, as an ordeal. By the time you get through to someone, panic has taken over and your imagination is working overtime.

What if Nemo was driving on the road near the bomb? He always drives on that road. What if he was driving at that second? Why isn't he picking up?

What if Lana was at the beach near the bomb? She always goes to that beach. She did say she was going to the beach that day. What if she is at that one? Why isn't she picking up?

And Sara, Maya's sister, lives right next to it. Did she hear it? Of course she did, it was just down her street. Why isn't she picking up? Why isn't her mom?

I called my sister and watched the news on TV at the same time. I looked at the police and the army walking through the rubble. Would they hear my sister's phone ringing and pick it up? I called and expect someone on TV to pick up my call.

I am tired. How long is one expected to fight? To stand up to the bully? What if the bully is so big, you can't actually see him in his entirety? You only catch a glimpse of an arm or a leg, and you worry about how big or complicated he is. What if the bully is really good at fooling you? Makes you think one thing and then hits you hard from behind, when you least expect it. That blow will bring you to your knees. It will knock the wind out of you, leaving you reeling to the floor, possibly landing in a sea of your own vomit.

I am not Superman. I am not Tarzan. Beirut and I, we have cracked and rebuilt ourselves so many times before. But how do I know if I can still keep doing it? For how long does it have to be this way?

Beirut, I want so many things from you. You give me a little, but you take so much in return.

Maya, I am not afraid of dying. We will get to live our dream somehow. Two eighty-year-old senile women, wearing funny hats, hunched backs, sitting on a balcony, drinking vodka and orange juice, listening to Dino, cracking jokes and wearing silk polka-dotted dresses. I will be there on the balcony. You will somehow be there. I will be waiting for you.

I remember the day the big war ended, last summer. Maya called me and screamed from the top of her lungs, "*It's over!*" She was laughing hysterically. I cried and laughed at the same time. I remember how my phone kept slipping off my ear because it was covered in tears and snot. I couldn't stop crying and laughing. I could see Maya through the phone. She was lying on her couch watching the news. Her beautiful hair was just starting to grow back. She looked like a baby duckling, a fine down. She was wearing her favorite turquoise T-shirt that read, "I Love Falafel". She had lost so much weight from the chemotherapy that her skin hung loose around her arms. Her pink pajama bottoms slipped past her hips. She had stopped wearing her bra months ago when she realized that she would not be leaving her home anytime soon. As she cried, "*It's over!*", she jumped up and down on her couch. Her arms and breasts flapped in the air. I could imagine this through the phone. She looked so funny with her beautiful bald head. We couldn't stop laughing.

How does it *end*? How does it *just* end? Is war like a machine? Do you just switch it off? How do you control man's rage? How do you make sure he takes his finger off the trigger? How can he be shooting with no remorse one minute, silent the next, and then in bed with his enemies, the next day? How do you pass word to him when he is still in the trenches? How does he know when to stop shooting?

Is ceasefire like the voice of God? Does it suddenly rain down from above, loud enough for the whole world to hear? Does it cleanse your heart and make you forget things? What happens the day after ceasefire? What do you do? Where do you go? Is your favorite bar still open? Will you work again? Will anyone want to spend money on your paintings? Can you watch reruns without feeling guilty? Will you find a new purpose to your life? One that means something? One that is worth living for?

2006 summer war: Zena's Blog

August 13, 2006 2:41am

on the eve of ceasefire, i have mixed emotions.
i am grateful that things are coming to an end.

however, the real work now lies ahead of us. its not just about rebuilding lives, country and morale. but it's also about moving forward positively on all sides.war instills hatred in people. we as human beings ... have to make sure that we don't fall into the vicious cycle of hate. we have to rise above the politics and speak as citizens of beautiful Mother Earth. i don't believe that we are born to hate. i believe that it is conditioned through things like fear, violence, oppression and misunderstanding.

one should not have to live in fear. one should not have to be subjected to violence.

it seems these days that violence and fear govern our lives. it is all over the TV and in the news ... but we should not let it. it is a disguise people use for their own selfish gains. the reality of life is love not fear. we have to remember that. life is beautiful ... it is like the never ending possibilities of youth ... it is like the first kiss ... remember that scene in The Matrix (the 3rd one), right at the end, when Neo and Trinity enter the Machine World ... they are flying

> their plane, holding hands ... love is guiding them through the war zone. then they shoot up into the sky, cutting away from the darkness, into the electric clouds ... fighting for their life ... then suddenly they get through it and they see Earth for what it really is: beautiful clear skies ... and then Trinity says "beautiful."
>
> i wonder if we can do that too.
>
> if there is one thing i have learned this past month, it is that life is so precious. in one second, your whole life could change. one day i was taking artwork down from a gallery about to send the paintings to their new respective owners ... the next morning, our airport was bombed and we were at war. just like that.
>
> life is so so precious.

One day, soon after the 2006 ceasefire, Maya decided that she had had enough. She realized that even though the war had ended, nothing really changed. There was so much stress. The knotted stomachs, the anxiety attacks, the fear of when it was all going to happen again. It was so easy the first time; it could be so easy the next. The nightmares began to pour in. People who were finally able to sleep found that the dream world held bigger fears than reality. The wish for a good night's sleep was gone. In reality lived broken-down bridges and buildings. In dream, all the dead people resided.

Maya saw through Beirut and realized it was all a scam. Maya broke her illusion when the mass burials from the war were being held. When all the bodies that had been left to rot were finally given peace. She saw the reality of bitter and tired citizens living in a fabricated dream world as they slowly began to catch all the new viruses going around, caused by the toxins coming out of the damaged buildings and the rotting bodies.

She saw that Beirut is just a pawn in a much bigger game. That we will always be her army whether we like it or not. That we will never have full control of our lives here. Beirut is a bitch and everyone wants his share.

The oil spill. The cloud of burning fuel that had covered Beirut for three weeks settled in Maya's lungs. Our neighbors managed to kill my best friend without even pointing a gun at her face. And who is next? And do they know they are poisoned as well? And the poor Mediterranean that we all love so much. Why did you scar her with your burning oil?

I did not realize that Maya was slipping away. She was at home and I was trying to clean oil from the beaches. I was breathing in fumes and she was breathing them out for me. She took in the toxins that were finding their way through my body. She took them off my hands, so that I could live. I should have been sitting right next to her. Nestled in her arms, watching reruns. But something kept me away. Maybe I knew she was leaving. Maybe it was nature's way. We gave up Maya so that we could have a future. Maybe I just did not want to face reality. Maybe it was easier to just throw myself into work, creating a dream that I was going to solve Lebanon's environmental problems.

This is the first June, July and August in Lebanon that I've lived without Maya. I wonder how long I am going to last. I think about my history. About my grandfathers and their ordeals in the New World. The schizophrenia and disappointment I felt with Amreeka throughout my many lifetimes. The feeling of drowning in the middle of the Atlantic. My great aunt, the infamous spy. About my grandmother once kidnapped from her village. About my mother who once burnt her dress. And my sister the paramilitary freedom fighter. My pill-popping friends. My sweet and troubled men.

I cannot help but feel that I am part of something much greater than this whore we call Beirut. That maybe Beirut is not what she seems to be. That, years from now, someone may read this and not even be able to even find Beirut on the map. She will be the lost city of Atlantis. She has built herself seven times, but how long can this charade go on? One day, it is all going to end. And when it does, it will be beautiful.

I will walk down to the beach. It will be clean. Maya will already be there, waiting for me. The two of us will sit down and watch the last sunset. Then come morning, my great-grandfather Nassif will rise from the Mediterranean and take my hand. He will apologize for letting go the first time and promise never to do the same again. We will walk into the water and I will not be afraid. Anything is better than war. Even death.

Beirut is too big to wear a wedding dress.

She cannot live forever.

Beirut, I love you.

"Why don't you have children?"

She finally broke her silence. I had spent a good half-hour walking her through my art exhibit. Explaining why I use glitter and how I refuse to allow my work to be labeled "kitsch" just because I use glitter. How I discovered, through a friend, that glitter is like God. Glitter reflects light.

We were walking through the installation when she finally decided to speak to me. I had made her take her shoes off. I wasn't sure I would be brave enough to ask her – women are fearful of exhibiting any bodily flaws and as you can imagine, I was hoping that her toes were intact and smelling like freshly cut roses that day.

The installation was a shrine dedicated to the Lebanese Civil War. It consisted of colored lights, pink, purple and gold fabric, glitter and incense. Like a life-size Day of the Dead altar. In the center of the room hung a sculpture I made of God. As I could not really depict what God looks like, I simply constructed the name out of cardboard. The cardboard was painted silver and on it I had glued pieces of broken glass that reflected light coming from a spotlight. It was a giant godly disco ball.

I don't think my guest noticed the sculpture as she walked

around, but when she finally decided to speak, she happened to stand right under it.

Her voice was sweet and not what I expected. Her Arabic not perfect, reminding me of myself. Her lips opened to speak.

"Why don't you have children?"

Of course you can imagine that this was not what I was waiting to hear and because of the absurdity of the question I found myself speechless.

Today, I question who was really talking to me. What if God was talking to me through my guest? Was someone communicating from the dead, through the shrine, into the sculpture of God and out of her sweet lips? I will never exactly know.

"I am afraid," I replied feeling embarrassed. I could not look into her eyes. My stare was directly to the floor. Nice and safe.

"Don't be afraid. They can help you with your work. In fact, they may be able to do it better. You never know. Just stop wasting time. You are not the first and you will not be the last woman to have children. In six months, I want a phone call from you telling me you are pregnant."

"Um ... yeah ... OK. If you want. I mean, I guess ... if I want. I mean ... uh ... we will see."

After she left I walked outside and sat on the stairs leading up to the gallery. The sky was a dark blue. It was May. It smelled like rain. Warm rain. The weather was definitely changing. There was a cool breeze making its way from the sea behind the gallery. I remember thinking that this could be the last week I would feel this breeze. Soon the oppressive summer heat would be upon us. I took off my shoes and rubbed the soles of my feet back and forth on the concrete step. It felt good. I zipped up my hot pink sweatshirt, lifted the hood up and covered my head, folded my arms across my chest, bent down and eventually the tears came. In the beginning they were soft and cold. They came out slowly. But then the damn broke. The questions, the unknown.

I called Mazen and demanded he come over to the gallery so I could tell him the story. At that moment, I wanted to make love to him. Right there in the gallery, I wanted to conceive. I wanted to and hoped that the experience with my wonderful guest would keep me from backing out, as I had usually done before. Do I listen to this woman who possibly could've been speaking from God? Should I simply go for it, right there and then? What to do? What to do?

Are you there God? It's me, Zena.

That night my husband and I slept at far ends of the bed. I did not dare touch him for fear of immaculate conception. Safe to say, at this very moment in time, I am still child-free. I want to see my lovely guest again, but I am afraid she will be disappointed with me. I can't handle that kind of pressure.

17

The last time we slept together, I knew it would be our last time. We almost didn't. He said it was wrong. I told him we were still husband and wife.

I gave it my best. I loved him with my whole body. I wanted to leave him with something he would never forget. Maybe it would help to make him feel bad after the divorce was final. I wanted him to feel bad later, by feeling good now.

I sat on top of him and took charge. My hips swirled. My hair hung over my face. I whispered. I licked his ears. I scratched his chest. I was almost another woman. The woman he could only dream of sleeping with. When the divorce would be final, I wanted him to remember this woman. And for the future, every time he would sleep with a new woman, I wanted to make sure he would remember me. That he would always see my face in hers.

He can't leave me. Not now. Not after everything that has happened.

I gave him my best. With my body that night, I gave him a woman he would never be able to forget. He may have decided to leave me, but I made sure he would never be able to forget me.

Beirut, give me strength.

Beirut, another man leaving.
Beirut, I blame you.
Beirut, I hate you.

18

We divorced.

Throughout the bitter screaming and blaming and finger pointing, there was a deep silence. My mouth was talking, but my ears were shut. There was only a muffled ringing in my head. Each time he opened his mouth to yell, I shut down. Hearing nothing. Only looking at his eyes. Blood-red monstrous eyes spitting fire. Eyes that once trapped my heart, now viciously ripped it to shreds. Eyes I once considered the soft color of honey, now dark and enraged. Empty, bottomless pit to hell. Hollow, like his heart. Selfish. Salivating. Rabid.

"You don't know me. You don't love me."

"Me? What about you. You don't know me. You stopped loving me."

"I never stopped loving you. I was just grieving. Am I not allowed to grieve?"

"You stopped loving me. You love Maya more than me."

"What? Maya is dead. What's wrong with you?"

"Maya is dead, and you still love her more than me. Now you love her more than when she was even alive. Her pictures are everywhere. You cry every night. Get drunk every night! All for Maya."

"I get drunk because of you, not because of her. Because you don't know how to love me. Because you let me drink, I drink. You never even try and stop me. It's like you want me to fuck up on purpose."

"Go and drink. I don't need to put up with this. You don't even touch me anymore. You haven't slept with me in months and it's been a year since Maya died. I waited, but nothing changed. I gave you your space in the beginning, but now I can't take it anymore. Men need to have sex. I need to have sex. If I don't sleep with you, my wife, I'm going to have to find it somewhere else."

"You already are. Stop threatening me. I know you're having an affair. I know about her."

"Zena, shut up. There is no one. We're just friends."

"No, no you're not. I've been spying on your text messages. Reading them when you're asleep. You are sleeping with her, aren't you?"

"Zena, if you don't stop this, I *will* start sleeping with her. And not only her. Everyone I can find. So stop it. Shut up. Don't push me. Be grateful I am not cheating on you."

Be grateful? Be grateful? Be grateful.

I was grateful that I was still alive. I closed my eyes and thought about Maya. Maya, I don't blame you. I am allowed to grieve. I am allowed to grieve.

I looked up at Mazen. This was it. I didn't want to be grateful to him anymore. And so, I asked.

I want a divorce.

I want a divorce.

I want a divorce.

I did it. I could never take those words away. They were out there – the thoughts materialized. And somehow, I knew I could be strong enough to go through with it. Beirut was listening in on the conversation; I knew I could rely on her to carry me.

How much are we supposed to put up with? Do we wait until he physically cheats on us before we call it quits? If we even do. What is the difference between an emotional cheat, a mental one or a physical one? Are they not all the same? How much bad behavior are we expected to put up with? How do we keep track, value and calculate it? How can we be assured that the other person is on the same level? Is it fair to expect so much from one person?

Divorce exists because marriage exists.

What if society were constructed differently? What if the system we live in now is just not good enough? The revolution is at our doorstep. All existing social structures are beginning to fail. All existing social structures will soon die out. The days of "Mother Mary" and "Father Bob" and "Son Dick" and "Daughter Jane" and their dog "Spot" will soon end. I declared it. I declared it the day I asked for my divorce.

If I am to fall, I am determined to bring the whole world down with me.

In Beirut, there are many broken homes. I always used to blame the war. Maybe it's not the war. Maybe Beirut is really OK. Maybe what is wrong are the systems imposed on her. Maybe she was not meant to put up with human beings and their silly ways. Silly humans who only want to take. Who want to be given things. Love. Security. Objects. Acknowledgment. Home. Lineage. Maybe that's why we get married in the first place. We perceive that through the union of marriage, we will be secured certain feelings, rights, objects, and of course coitus.

Is it impossible these days to just float? And breathe? Not plan anything?

Just lay there?

Calm.

Serene.

There was a time when it seemed possible.

In Nigeria, I used to fill my bathtub and submerge myself up to my ears. The water was always a rusty orange color, but I never worried or cared about that. Once my ears were under water, all I could hear was my heartbeat, and absolutely nothing else mattered. Everything was silence. Everything else, all the noise, was literally drowned out. My life would somehow cease to exist. I was only floating. My timeline would break down into events. Events that did not connect, but rather appeared as instances, or flashes, with every heartbeat. Hierarchy in all its forms would become meaningless. Nothing was more important than the other. One event was equal to the next.

The event of my marriage is equal to the event of my divorce.

The thirty-four-day summer war, equal to twenty-five years of civil war.

Rumi equal to Shams.

Zena equal to Maya.

19 

While all the foreign papers are still writing about the war that took place two summers ago, there have been three new ones that have happened since, but gained zero media coverage.

The war in my heart.

The war on my streets.

The war to keep Beirut.

The other day on Hamra Street, I was on my way to a meeting when I ran into a gun. I had just walked out of my new apartment, feeling independent and strong. The divorce had not gotten the best of me. No way. Beirut, I can still take you on.

I walked down Hamra on my way to a meeting. In Beirut, cops carry semi-automatic machine guns, not pistols. He was walking a few paces in front of me. His gun was strapped over his right shoulder, pointing down. It was swinging back and forth with every step that he took. I veered a little to the left. It dawned upon me that if he was not careful, if his gun was not on safety, it could have easily shot a bullet in my direction. I didn't want to take any chances, so I veered to the left. Without noticing, I ran into another cop standing on the left. I was so fixated on the one in front of me, I failed to see this new one. As hard as I tried to avoid the first gun, the second one ran right into me. Right into my crotch.

Here we go again. Beirut and my crotch.

But this time I didn't have Maya to bail me out.

Guns. Since the summer war there have been so many guns. And people have stopped falling in love.

Perverts, cocked rifles, ready to shoot, ready to penetrate their targets with their trajectories, armed, ready, sweaty, smelly, hairy, moldy.

Rubbed his gun against my crotch

I opened my mouth to say something.

Offensive: could get me into trouble, what if it was a mistake?

Polite: I would be letting him get away with it, what if it was on purpose.

To cry, I would lose.

He did it on purpose, I know he did. Since the last war, security on the streets has upgraded. The Amreekans have been sending us all their used weapons, trucks and tanks. They have been sending the U.S. Special Forces to train our charming young men. Men who previously would never stop a pretty girl on the street now create blockades for them. Men who previously would bow their heads in respect now swing their guns at them.

He did it on purpose, I know he did.

Pervert.

They all are. Those cops. Our old ones wore blue and gray. But these new ones are dark blue. They are the specially-trained new-and-improved security forces.

Perverts they are, for throwing their guns at me. For blockading my street, their presence on every corner. We never had these kinds of men before. Their bodies are from here – their shells. But on the inside, a seed has been planted and a new kind of monster is growing.

Perverts.

They all are, with their guns in their hands – "click, clack, lock 'n' load".

These days when you give directions on how to get from one place to another, you use tanks as references. When giving street directions we casually mention a left turn, not at the first tank, but the second. How easy it has become to say such things.

The other day, Nour went to a party at the Amreekan embassy. Since my divorce, she had not left my side. I think Maya sent her to me. I think Beirut sent her to me. When one door closes, ten others open. Is that not the saying?

Nour went to the embassy. It was a pre-Saint Patrick's Day bash. She met a nice guy. She said he was polite and that it was good to meet polite men for a change. He asked for her number and called her a few days later. They chatted for a while and then he asked her if she would like to meet up for a movie. She told him that she was not really into Hollywood flicks, but that she could find a thoughtful independent film if he was interested.

He said "Yes".

She said "Good".

But then there was the condition. He could not leave the embassy – she would have to come over. The Amreekan embassy is about a twenty-minute drive outside Beirut, or forty-plus if there's traffic. And there is always traffic. The embassy is situated in a Christian enclave up in the mountains. Once you get up the mountain, there is only one road and it leads straight to the embassy. Along the way, there are at least half a dozen checkpoints. It is a fortress, not an embassy. A medieval fortress they use to protect themselves against the evil and violent Musalman. Calling it an embassy is giving it too much credit.

Nour came over for a visit soon after and asked for advice – should she go and see him there?

Silence.

It's so hard to be objective about Amreekans these days, let alone men in general.

"Nour, they are guests in our country. But he is 'not allowed' to walk around without his two bodyguards and armored vehicles. You need a man who respects you. Who respects your culture. If you are OK living in Beirut, he should be OK to come and visit you. Why should it be good enough for you and not for him? I am sick and tired of these double standards. Tell him to go fuck himself. If he is too afraid to take you out for a decent coffee in Beirut, don't waste a second of your time with him."

"Zena, it's not that black and white. He's a nice guy. And you know that all foreigners have been warned to take precautions. He works with the embassy, for God's sake! They are afraid he could be kidnapped. I think it's OK that he asked me to come over."

"Maybe you're right, but really ... when was the last time someone was kidnapped in Beirut? That's just so old school. We are a thriving cosmopolitan city now. No one kidnaps anyone anymore! That was the '80s and we are now in the new millennium. Tactics have changed. Evolved. Kidnappings don't work anymore. The Amreekan embassy warns about kidnappings not because they care about their workers, but because they don't want to pay all that money to get them back. It's all about money. Remember the summer war – they told all their citizens here that they would have to pay the government back for their evacuation. They had to sign a paper that said that they would be charged for their evacuation once they reached their homes. They are just trying to save money and not their people."

"I know, but you know what I mean. There are rules. He has to follow them."

"Nour, I'm sorry if I am sounding so harsh. I'm just so upset because one day the Amreekans are sending their bombs to Israel to attack us with, and thirty-four days later, they come to us wanting to be our friends. They send their hi-tech special forces to train our beautiful men and turn them into animals. They send their weapons of all shapes and sizes and we sit there and eat it up. This Sam guy might be a really nice guy, but he represents the monster. I will not allow you to go into the lion's den. If he really likes you, let him come to Beirut. Let him cross over and taste our thick coffee and our sweets dripping in honey. To hell with filter coffee and Twizzlers!"

"Zena, you're really upset. Did something happen today? I feel like this is about more than just Sam."

"I am OK physically, but not emotionally. I can't even walk on my own streets now. There are tanks and guns everywhere. And the fucked up thing is that they are not even ours. I mean, they are ours, but we didn't make them. And now I can't even walk or drive without them being pointed in my face. I left New York because I was sick and tired of being racially targeted. I thought I would finally be safe in Beirut. Beirut, where we are all crazy and it's accepted, and there is no need to point fingers or guns at anyone. But now, New York has followed me here."

"You're right. If he really likes me, he has to come to Beirut and pick me up in a regular car."

"Nour, that's not what I meant, but yes, he does. Already, he is an imposition. And we, we are not like the Japanese."

"Zena! That's not very nice."

"No, I'm serious. No offense to the Japanese, but really, how much humiliation can one nation take? The Japanese had the bomb dropped on them and they were so quick to forgive. They were put into concentration camps and racially profiled for years after the war. And now ... they are best friends with the Amreekans. They gave up their army. They let the Amreekans build an air force base on one of their islands, whose people are now subsequently losing their beautiful ancient traditional culture to hamburgers and milkshakes. These Amreekans, they throw their bombs on us, via our neighbors, and now they send us special task forces to beef up our security. Why? So that the next time there is a war they will say, 'Oh sorry, we tried to help, but it seems you people are hopeless'. No ,Nour, we are more than this. They offer us green card lotteries like we are hungry dogs and then question us for eight hours when we land in their country. They take our fingerprints. Photograph us. Take notes. Screen us because of our names. They sell bombs to our neighbors and then they train our men and then they invite us to come live in their country and spend our hard-earned money on their economy so that they can make even more bombs to sell to our neighbors to drop on our people. What kind of schizophrenia is that? No. No, we don't have to take it."

"OK. Maybe I shouldn't call him back. I definitely won't go over."

"Oh Nour! I am so sorry. I know that he's probably a really nice guy, but he is employed by the monster and you have to remember that. I am sure he comes from a great family and maybe they even have one of those wooden houses with the white fences and a golden dog. But still, he serves the beast. Maybe he goes to church every Sunday. Maybe he has the nicest friends and they all respect their parents and have a very giving outlook on life. But if he has chosen to side with the government that is killing our people, then I don't think he's the right one for you."

"So, I shouldn't call him."

"No. I don't think you should."

"Shit. I haven't had sex in so long. I was hoping things could work out."

"But for getting hassle-free sex, I think you're losing a lot."

"How? What do you mean?"

"For example: when you make a Lebanese man come, you know that he really really feels it. Because of all the stress we live under, you know that it was totally worth it. Like, it wasn't sex for the sake of sex. It was sex that affirms our existence. When we come, we are alive. We are real. We are not dead. For every ejaculation, there is a celebration of life. Nothing is taken for granted."

"OK, Zena, enough poetry. Do you think we need sex in order to survive?"

"No. We need sex to know we are alive. Being alive and surviving are two different things. I don't want to survive, I want to be alive.

"But then again, I mean, today I am saying these things to you, but ask me tomorrow and I may say completely different things. That is the nature of this land. One day I swear off sex, the next I'm crying because I don't have any. One day I stand on my balcony and wish I could hug the city in front of me, the next I keep my shutters closed and stay home all day. This is what Beirut is becoming."

"Beirut or you?"

"No, Beirut. I am just her messenger. When she is insecure, then so am I. When she is at her best, I am glowing. To live here, in this city, is to have blind faith. You can't think or analyze. And despite it being a love-hate relationship, you have to always move with your heart."

"But Zena, the whole world is yours for the taking. Why do you limit yourself to being here, trapped under something you can't control? You have other options, you know."

"No, I don't. I can't leave. I have never been happy anywhere else. In other cities and continents, they have found ways to keep you entertained. Ways to distract you through simulated happiness. Despite the mess, I feel that here, I am free. At least when I am miserable I know that I am. It reminds me that I am alive. I'd rather be miserable than artificially happy."

"Why does everything have to be so extreme with you?"

"It's not. This is our world today.. Look at the Chinese people and what they have to deal with. They have become the victims of our consumption. Soon they will stop seeing the sun, which is already beginning to happen. And then, they will have to start paying for containers of clean air in order to breathe. They are paying the price for the things we want to have. They are the ones living in a city beyond their control. I'm doing just fine here in Beirut."

"But what about all the pollution here? Things we can't see. There is so much cancer now."

"I don't want to talk about cancer."

"Zena, don't start this. You have to accept what happened to Maya. All the chemicals from the bombs our neighbors dropped on us. All the toxic fumes and tar from the oil spill. The nuclear waste the Europeans paid us to take off of their hands while we were having our civil war. It's all in our air, in our water, in our vegetables, and in our soil. Maya breathed it. I am breathing it. And so are you."

"I can't deal with this now. There is already so much. I just want to get through one day without thinking of war, disease, bombs, instability, depression, anxiety, stress, politics, and cancer. It is so much easier to forget than to deal with these things."

"But you are always complaining about how everyone forgets. How the civil war was forgotten. How accountability has been erased."

"Maybe. Maybe I have. Maybe this is what happens in Beirut. Maybe this is really the only way to live."

"I don't know. I just try not to think of these things. Not really forgetting, but just not thinking so much."

A few minutes of silence passed between us. I took Nour's hand in my own. "I think you should call him. Fuck it. Life is too short. Who knows, maybe he's the one. Your 'Prince Charming'. Maybe it's your destiny to leave us here and live in one of those TV houses and drink Gatorade and bake cookies."

"You think I should call? It's not really about sex, you know that."

"I know. We're all so desperate to get into something that is more than Beirut. Something that will take our minds off of things. Something to believe in. Love. Love is the only thing that gets us through. Love is what makes us live. Live and not survive."

"It does, doesn't it? I just want to be in love again."

"Me too. When I am in love, I don't see anything else around me. Beirut becomes so animated and inspiring. My life becomes worth living. I don't feel like I'm wasting time. I am always worried that I am going to die tomorrow. I can't die without love in my heart. That would be too cruel."

"He is very polite you know. That must mean something."

"I think it does. You know those Amreekans are really nice people. It's just their government that sucks. But governments change all the time. And love – love could last forever."

20 ♡

Makram.

I used to write to him every time I came home drunk. What is it that compels you to fall in love with someone? I think most of the time it's because you see a little of yourself in them. Or you see the aspects of the person you would like to be. Falling in love can be an ego trip. By loving Makram I was loving myself. There are some people who bring out the best in you.

I always contemplated telling him, but knew that if I ever did, our friendship would end. Since the very first time we spoke, our relationship was based on what was unsaid. Our comfort was in the silence.

The gestures of the hand.

The blink of an eye.

The hunched shoulders. The quiet smiles. The ink stains on my finger, the nicotine on his.

The late-night alcohol-induced letters.

In reality, we were uncomfortable around each other. In altered states, it was bliss.

I purposefully put Makram on a pedestal. He represented a Beirut I always wanted, but could never have. He lived through the war, the civil war, and with so much pain. The scars were visible on his tired face. In his gestures and demeanor. He knew Beirut in her brute strength. Intimately. And it haunted him. Makram, in my eyes, was a rose among weeds. Tall. Different. Beautiful. On the outside, he looked twice his age, he looked battered and withered. But if you could get close enough to him, you would see that his body, his frame, was a façade. It was a disguise to deter Beirut. It was a trick to blend in. To hide. To be overlooked every time Beirut cast down her evil wand. If you could get close enough to Makram, you would be able to see that his eyes always burned a bright green and hazel.

In overcrowded buses and taxis he always had his eyes closed. While standing at checkpoints, he always looked down. While pushing his way down the street, he never made eye contact. He never even dared to look up into the sky. Just in case she saw him.

But I did.

Our friendship began when our eyes locked for the first time. In a room full of a hundred people, we both looked up at each other at the same time and neither one backed down. We just kept looking.

The week we first met, I thought I had found my one true love. I suddenly kept running into him everywhere. We would look at each other, try to start a conversation, fail and then blush. Sometimes he would sit beside me, light up his cigarette and smoke in silence. Sometimes I would walk over and ask a random question to which his reply would always be gray. Sometimes I gave him pebbles. Sometimes he gave me rolls of film for the camera that never left my side. Once I gave him a black ink pen. A "0.5 Staedtler Pigment Liner". Once he gave me a smile, the one that says he might be in love too.

When Makram's long hair began to fall out, he grew a beard. It was self-defense. The longer his beard was, the greater the energy field that protected him from the daily barrage of war, kidnappings, traffic, and disappointments. The more hair he grew out, the more of him there was to assert his place in this city. He was already well over six feet tall, but his beard gave him an added advantage.

His apartment was situated in a part of town that was densely built, a concrete jungle with one building crawling on top of the other. Concrete poured on top of concrete. The windows were small in order to keep the chaos outside. His whole family lived in the tiny apartment. In Lebanon, it is not unusual for a man to live with his parents. The move-out usually happens only when there is marriage.

I often wondered what it would be like to be married to him.

Would we finally learn how to speak to each other? Up until the last time I saw him, it was still the same story. The intensity of the pain in his eyes always pushed me to behave like a clown. Happy. Bouncy. Shallow. Maybe if we were to meet today, it could be different. I am no longer afraid of pain. I know I would be able to look at him without blushing. I know I would be able to find the right words. Makram, if you are reading this, I want you to know that I have found the right words to say to you. I won't behave like a young girl. I will be a woman. The woman that you need me to be. I am calm now. I am ultramarine blue and deep. If you give me a chance, I have so much to give.

In the summers he used to walk around barefoot and topless in his home. Clad only in jeans at sunset, his habit was to take out his *oud* and play to the traffic below in an attempt to tame his city. His neighbors all loved him for it. It was the only time of the day when they could feel that they had not been beaten. Um Khaled, who lived below him, grew a jasmine bush in his honor. While he provided her with beautiful music, she felt that the only thing she could do in return was to provide the scent to his melodies. It was a small paradise.

He never officially invited me over to his home. I just happened to tag along with a friend one day. He was very surprised to see me. I pretended everything was normal. A few days later, I invited myself over. Alone. His mother opened up for me and welcomed me in. She didn't ask who I was. She just casually pointed to the balcony and said that Makram was already out there. Maybe she was used to it. Maybe he always had girls over. I walked over and sat down on the cushion by his feet. He was playing his *oud* and did not stop to say hello. But he did smile. I smiled back and pulled out my sketchbook. He played. I drew. We never spoke. I kept inviting myself over.

One afternoon, I noticed that his chest hairs were beginning to turn gray. At first I thought it was the reflection of the sun. I put my sketchbook down on the floor and imagined myself reaching out to touch his chest. I wanted to stroke his hairs with the back of my hand. I wanted to caress them and tell them that it was OK that they had turned gray because it was not their fault.

I put down the sketchbook and imagined myself getting up and walking towards him. I imagined that I would stand right behind him. I imagined that I would put my lips on his balding head and gently cover it with kisses. Slowly. Each kiss, deliberate. As he sat cross-legged and played, I would tell his head that it was all going to be OK. I imagined that I would run my lips across his head. That his tiny hairs would embrace my lips and tell me about how upset they were. Upset because Beirut had stolen their youth. That they were once long and lush, but eventually had to give up because Beirut was too stressful.

I imagined that I put my sketchbook down and walked over to him. I would stand behind him and gently put my hand on the nape of his neck. I would bend down and place my cheek on his neck. Breathing slowly. To the rhythm of his *oud*. I would notice that his shoulders had tiny freckles on them. I imagined that he would then stop playing, abruptly, and place his hand over mine. That he would put his *oud* down on the floor and pull me to him. I imagined that I would then straddle him and sit on his lap. I would cup his face in my hands and look into his eyes. His honey-colored eyes would then compel me to speak; words that I have to say only because they sound so beautiful and not because their definitions pertain to our current scenario in any way, shape, or form. Words like, chrysanthemum.

Abundance.

Sunrise.

Fringe.

Fuchsia.

Indigo.

Linger.

After pouring words out in random order, I would lean in to kiss his lips. He, of course, would not move. He may barely respond. But he would, nevertheless, let me.

Kiss him.

Makram, of course kept playing, oblivious to my imaginings.

He was absolutely lovely.

I didn't pick up my book again. It was dark. Makram continued playing until the moon came out. I sat still, afraid to break his concentration. Maybe he forgot I was there. But I imagined that he didn't. I imagined that every note was struck for me.

That while his eyes were closed, he imagined us sharing a glass of wine.

That while his eyes were closed, he imagined us sitting on the tip of the moon. Looking down at Beirut. Feeling safe. Our bodies entwined in an embrace that was bare and honest. Legs wrapped around arms around hands and hair and cracks and cum.

Maybe one day I will tell him about these daydreams.

Maybe one day I will drink enough and purge myself.

Or maybe it is better to keep quiet.

Because the pain of unrequited love is more exquisite than the instant gratification of sex.

Living in Beirut compels us to opt-out for instant gratification. Through sex, we beat death. Through sex, we can exist. But, Makram and I, our story is different. By not having sex, we were different and we continue to be different.

But ask me today and I will say Beirut has a fucking point. Because one night with Makram would have been worth all those endless Sufi summer nights.

21

I am living in an apartment where I have to plan at least two hours ahead if I am going to take a shower.

I like that. I like that I cannot take anything for granted. Sitting here, under my blaring white energy-saving fluorescent bulb, I have never been so happy. Here, everything around me is good, because it's simple. I like that I know exactly where the box of painkillers is because it is exactly where I left it. I know that my green shoes are in my left closet and the burgundy steel toes are in the right. I know how much gas is left in the cooker, because I know exactly how much cooking I've done. I know how much hot water to heat. I know that my white shirt is still in the laundry hamper. I know when the plants were watered last. I know that I can drink alone with no one to judge me but the angel on my shoulder. I know when Tapi needs to be walked because I fed her and walked her last. I know that I can stay at home all day and no one will pass by because they think that I'm doing fine. I know, because I trick them into thinking that.

I know that if I read old emails from ex-lovers, I will get depressed. But I know that there's no one to stop me so I open up the computer anyway.

I know that I can hold Maya's picture in my hands and cry for as long as I need. I know that I won't be interrupted and that I won't have to explain myself. I know that I can put her picture on the pillow beside me and fall asleep knowing that no one will walk in and catch me. I know that I can talk to her out loud without embarrassment. I know that I don't have to worry about people thinking that I'm emotionally unbalanced, because there is no one there to hear me.

I know that I will have a hard time sleeping tonight. Because I know that I will be sleeping alone.

But I also know that things will improve, because they can't always be like this.

I have found myself thinking about my Grandpa Mohammad a lot these days.

Was life this difficult back then? How did people deal with loneliness and disappointment before they had Xanax and the comedy channel? How did he deal with the stress and pressure of trying to make his life count for something? How did he feel when his home was occupied? All the rejection and disillusionment I've faced in my life, barely comes close to what he experienced.

As it is with family tradition in the Arab world, respectful stories of our elders are passed by word of mouth from generation to generation. Every time my father told me the story of my Grandpa Mohammad's journey to the New World, I felt a sense of pride and nostalgia in his voice. I know that deep down inside, he hoped that I would remember everything word for word, and pass it down to my children. But the truth is – to me – Grandpa Mohammad's stories seem so removed.

Sometimes, I even feel slightly repulsed by them.

It is impossible for someone to live their whole life with their head held high. Always making the right decisions. Never falling. Never crying.

I am much more fascinated by my grandfather's mistakes, those that my father would never share with me. However, I find it easy, looking at my own life, to guess at some of his mistakes. Namely, the burden of trying to make his life count for something amid the humiliation of rejection.

When I retell the story of Grandpa Mohammad to my children, I will do it differently. I won't make him a saint, the way my father does. I might even disgrace him a little. And it's not because I don't love him. It's because I know he is human. I will tell my children a story they can relate to. I will want my children to have a fair chance at life. I will want them to grow up without the burdens I assumed. They will be allowed to make mistakes.

If I were to retell the story of Grandpa Mohammad, it would go a little something like this.

When Grandpa Mohammad was only thirteen years old, he decided that life had to have more meaning than his work at our family farm. After convincing his mother to let him explore what the world had to offer, he made his way out of the backstreets of the Ottoman Levant and headed down towards the port city of Beirut. Little did he know then that it would be twenty years before he would return home.

Upon arrival in Beirut, he decided that he was going to catch a ship and head off to the New World. He decided to go to Amreeka.

Making his way through Beirut's bustling alleys he came across the strangest noises. He thought it was a cat in heat, but it was actually a woman moaning. He thought the thudding of a rickety wooden bed from the floor above was thunder. The deep sigh of relief from a man's throat, he believed to be God talking to him.

"Ya Mohammad!" it cried.

"Ya Mohammad!" it sounded.
"Ya Mohammad!" it roared.
And then: silence.

Grandpa Mohammad *(In a great state of panic)*: Dear God, I hear and obey you. What would you make of me? How can I serve you? Please forgive me. I meant not to leave my mother, but you see I had no choice.

Mohammad fell to his knees and awaited his punishment. It came to him in the form of a bucket of cold water, which he mistook to be a thousand daggers piercing his heart. He waited for the tunnel of light only to find a beautiful redhead leaning out the window.

Redhead *(Very angry, twisting a lock of hair)*: You. Who do you think you are?

Grandpa Mohammad *(In disbelief, squeaks out)*: I am Mohammad.

Redhead *(Now very annoyed):* Ya Mohammad, what in God's name do you think you're doing outside my window?

Grandpa Mohammad: Please forgive me, but I heard the voice of God calling my name. Please tell Him I am here. I am ready. I admit to making a mistake of leaving my dear mother, and now, I am ready to pay the penalty. I am here for repentance.

Redhead *(Now finding her sense of humor)*: So what are you saying? That my husband is God?

Grandpa Mohammad *(Still with his arms raised up, bows his head down.)*

Redhead *(Tired of this game, retreats inside)*

Enter God.

God *(Hairy chested with a hazy look in his eyes):* Eh boy, what do you want? Who sent you?

Grandpa Mohammad *(Quivering, slowly begins to lower his arms)*: My mother, Sitt Abir.

Redhead *(Scathing)*: Khalil, who the Hell is Abir? What whore have you been visiting? It is not enough that I put out for you every damn day. Twice a day, like clockwork, for the past fifteen years? What kind of a sexual monster are you? What kind of a beast? May God strike you down if that boy is your son!

(The sound of a breaking object, possibly a plate or a lantern)

God a.k.a. Khalil *(Retreating from the window, in a panic)*: Oh, dearest sweetest love of my life, I have no idea who he is!

Grandpa Mohammad *(With virtue and pride, imploring, shouting)*: I am the son of Abir!

Redhead *(Screaming)*: Khalil, who is Abir??

God a.k.a. Khalil *(Now back at the window)*: You little shit. You have ruined my afternoon fuck. Go and tell that Abir woman that I will have none of you. You are not my son. I don't even know an Abir!

Grandpa Mohammad: Dear God, are we not all your children? Please dear God, if I am not yet dead, direct me at your will and I will obey and follow.

Redhead: Khalil, stop wasting my time and tell me the truth! Is the boy out of his mind or is he really your son?

Grandpa Mohammad: Wife of God, if I may, my father died when I was very young. My mother has never set foot in Beirut. I do not know what you are talking about. All I know is that one minute I was alone in this great city and then the next, I hear the voice of God calling my name three times: Mohammad, Mohammad, Mohammad!

Redhead *(Now understanding the mix-up, chuckles to herself)*: Just throw him some coins and come back to bed. It is clear that this boy is out of his mind.

God a.k.a. Khalil *(Throws two silver piasters out the window)*: Take this money and make something out of yourself. And when you're done, give my regards to your mother. *(To his wife)* We are going to move out of this city. Everyone here is crazy!

Grandpa Mohammad: God. Bless you. I will never fail you. *(Scurries off)*

It would be so much easier to tell Grandpa Mohammad's story that way. With humor and sarcasm. In the spirit of Beirut and her dark side. I would then tell my children that with his first silver piaster, Grandpa Mohammad ate well and did not forget his promise to God. His first pledge was to take on God's earthly name. The one that he had overhead God's wife call him. And that is how our family acquired the last name el Khalil. I would then tell them that Grandpa Mohammad of the Khalil spent his second silver piaster on his ticket to the New World.

Grandpa Mohammad making his way to the docks would join the line for the ship heading to New York via Marseilles. His ticket, firm in his hand; his back, stiff; demeanor, serious; balls, slightly itchy; eyes, reddish. However, what Grandpa Mohammad did not know was that during his slumber in the shadows of the alleys of Beirut, he had contracted pink eye.

When it was his turn to embark, he would be stopped by a

menacing force of power that had rotten teeth, but a well trimmed beard.

"Son, you cannot board my ship with your pink eye."

"Sir, I have my ticket here in my hand. It says nothing of pink eye."

"Son, I will ask you to kindly step aside. No sick people are allowed to travel to Amreeka. But if you want, you can take the ship that is docked on the other end of the port. It is for sick people. It will not take you to Amreeka, but it will take you to Mexico. Mexico is OK for sick people, not Amreeka. Do you understand? From Mexico you can walk to Amreeka. It will take you a long time, but if you really want to get to Amreeka, I am guessing that it will not be a problem for you."

Grandpa Mohammad, having no other choice, would get on the sick people boat. He had once walked from his village in the south of Lebanon to his uncle's in the far north. It took him a week. Mexico, he would assume, couldn't be longer.

After sixteen years of roaming around Mexico, Grandpa Mohammad would find himself as penniless as the first day he arrived. My father's version of the story states that on the night of Grandpa Mohammad's return to Lebanon, a group of bandits invaded his store. Having no other choice, he welcomed them in. After he saw to it that they were happily eating and drinking, he informed them that he was going to sleep, but they were welcome to stay for as long as they liked. His only request was for them to please remember to close the door behind them. After all, there were bandits out there.

With that, he scurried up to the attic and pretended to be asleep. In and out of his deceptive snoring, he overhead the bandits plotting to kill him. Within the blink of an eye, Grandpa Mohammad decided to abscond. Scooping up whatever he could carry, which was not really that much, he leaped out the attic window, turned his back on Mexico forever.

In all honesty, I think my grandfather just broke down. I don't think there were any bandits. I think my grandfather was genuinely homesick and tired. I think he was heartbroken, ashamed, lost, insecure, and fucking lonely.

He never made it to Amreeka.

We spend our whole lives trying to get somewhere and never realize that we might actually be there already. In our day and age, it seems that nothing is good enough anymore. There is always more to be had. We have options. We have planes. We have wi-fi. We have divorce.

Life is messy.

Here in my new apartment, I have learned not to be afraid of the dark. I can sit all alone in the dark now. I can sleep alone in the dark. I can type in the dark and even cook. I don't like it, though. I really don't like it. It puts me in a state of suspension – a state of nothingness. Of drifting and letting go. Here in my silence, I can hear my breath. And the breath materializes into thoughts and the thoughts become words and before I know it I find myself sprawled on my sofa crying because I'm so lonely. I don't want to say it, but I do. And they are the only words that are formed in this darkness.

22

But what is it that defines a place? The way it looks … the way it acts … or the time and space it falls into? Maybe it's the stories we will remember later.

My new apartment is a microcosm of Beirut. It is located in a divided Muslim neighborhood. If I leave my apartment from the front door, I am in the hands of Al Mostaqbal, the Sunni pro-Amreekan militia. If I decide to take the back door from the kitchen, it's Berri and Musa all the way – representatives of the Shiite pro-Iranian Amal militia. These two Muslim parties are currently opposed to each other. Funny how a tiny apartment can divide the neighborhood like that.

During the civil war in the '80s, this area was a Communist party stronghold. Everyone who lived in my building somehow sided with the Communist-Hamra Street ideology. These old fighters are now retired, but still pursue their age-old ideologies, but in new and improved ways. They now own bars, write in newspapers and even run cultural organizations.

My building is old, has high ceilings and green shutters at the windows. I live on the first floor, which means that the whole neighborhood can see what color underwear I am wearing.

I wonder what they think of me? The divorced woman who has just moved in. Who lives alone with her dog, that filthy creature. The woman who is seen drinking on her balcony every night. It must be wine because she drinks it out of a wine glass. Or maybe it's vodka because sometimes the sound of ice clinking can be heard all the way down the street. If I cough, the whole neighborhood knows I'm sick. I wonder what would happen if I were ever to invite a man over. I wonder if my sister will be able to hear us upstairs. Or my neighbors below me.

I hear my downstairs neighbors all the time. Only last night they were arguing. But it was too muffled to figure out what was going on. This morning I went over to Um Tarek's for the scoop. Um Tarek, my Egyptian neighbor, lives on the second floor. She is our resident cat woman. Her door is always open and she takes care of the stray cats in our neighborhood. Some of which fell in love with Um Tarek and decided to make their home with her. Some decided they were just happy with the free meals and just stop to visit every now and then. Um Tarek has saved over one thousand cats in our neighborhood since she arrived in 1974.

I walked up the stairs to her apartment, stepping over puddles of cat pee. Um Tarek's door was open. I knocked and asked if I could come in.

"Come in, ya Zena. Come in, I just got out of the shower, please give me one minute. Sit, I'm coming," Um Tarek's hoarse voice called from inside.

"OK, thanks." I gently tiptoed over some cats sprawled across the entrance to her home. "Please excuse me, my dears, I'm just coming to pay your aunty a visit."

I plopped down on her couch, just missing a small white kitten curled up under a throw pillow. Um Tarek's apartment was what one could call an organized mess. In front of me was a dark wood bookshelf that was littered with pictures of her children and her cats from over the years. There was a small vase with big white plastic flowers that kind of looked like giant jasmine. To my right, the plants from her balcony spilled into the living room.

"Um Tarek, your plants are growing into the living room. Do you leave your windows open all the time?"

"Of course, I have to. For the cats. Otherwise, they can't come home."

"But don't you get cold in the winter?"

"I do but what can I do? Someone has to help these poor creatures." Um Tarek towel dried her hair with one arm, while she talked. It was very curly and a beautiful shade of red from the henna that she had recently used. She was wearing a plum-colored bathrobe and turquoise flip-flops. Under her other arm was a small gray cat that had apparently just showered with her. She fell onto the couch near me.

"Your living room is becoming a jungle," I told her.

"I know. The cats like it better this way. It feels like they are still out on the streets. It's important for them to feel that, otherwise they will get sick and die. If they feel that they are indoors or trapped, they go crazy. The woman who had the apartment before you, Nibal, had a cat she kept indoors the whole time. He was on so much medication. When she moved, I took him in. First I made him sleep on the streets for a few weeks. This built up his immunity. Then I let him come and visit every now and then. Poor baby was so skinny. He didn't even know how to catch his own food. Now, he's as strong as a horse. Doesn't need his medicine anymore. And he comes and goes as he pleases." Her eyes turned to the gray cat that was now nestled on her thighs trying to dry himself against the bathrobe. "This one," she said, pointing down to the cat, "this one I am worried about. He has electricity in his head. Every few days he has a crisis and goes mad. This morning he had a bad one and ran up and down the apartment like he was possessed or something. He scratched a lot of the other cats and then ran around and around in circles until he just collapsed. I found him here on the floor and he was covered with his own shit and piss and white saliva. When he calmed down, I took him in to shower with me. Poor thing."

"You mean he's epileptic?"

"I don't know what that is. The neighbors are saying he is cursed and that God has decided to give him this fate. Soon he may die. I have to take care of him for as long as I can. God sent him through my door."

"Um Tarek, a lot of people live their whole lives with epilepsy and you wouldn't even know it. There is medication for it. We can get some for the cat."

"No. No. It would never work. Have you ever tried to feed a cat medication? It's almost impossible. This one, he was born in the streets and he will die there. It's too late to domesticate him. This is his fate. Trying to feed him medicine would be an insult."

"Then why don't we put him to sleep and end his misery?" I asked.

"God forbid! Zena, how can you even suggest such a thing? We are all born into this world with our handicaps. It is our challenge and destiny to live with them. We don't know what's going on in this cat's head. We cannot judge for him. Only God will judge."

"I'm sorry, Um Tarek." I looked sheepishly down at my feet. "You are right." There was no point in arguing because no one could ever intervene between Um Tarek and her spiritual connection to her cats. "Um Tarek, did you hear the neighbors arguing last night?"

"Oh my God, Zena, you heard it too?"

"How could I not? I live right above them. Do you know what was going on?"

"Zena, Zena, Zena ... you are still new to this neighborhood and there are still many stories you don't know about." She chuckled, stroking the gray cat that was now almost dry. "The couple who live below you are miserable people. Um Adnan, the mother, has been having an affair with a boy younger than her son, and her husband just found out. Actually, he doesn't know for sure, but every now and then he accuses her."

Um Adnan was a stout woman in her fifties. Recently deciding that life was too short and she wanted to enjoy it more, she decided to start up an affair after being loyal to her husband for over twenty years. She cut her hair very short, bleached it a blondish orange and went out on the prowl to find herself a lover. She could be seen walking up and down our street in tight bicycle shorts and a casual T-shirt. She wanted to look young and hip, showing off the curves of marriage on her hips. She didn't care that girls these days were stick thin. Her body, she was convinced, was what men really wanted. A soft place to fall into. Breasts the size of mountains, to get lost in. Skin that stretched for endless miles, to forever caress.

Um Adnan on the prowl didn't have to go far. A week after she cut her hair, her husband hired a young Syrian migrant worker to do some construction on their apartment. Syrian labor is very cheap and Abu Adnan was happy he got so lucky with Youssef. Youssef had just arrived from Aleppo and was still very green. Abu Adnan promised to provide room and board in exchange for Youssef's services. Youssef agreed and was hired on the spot.

That very night, Um Adnan crept out of her bed at night and

stole into the kitchen for a peek at this new member of their family. Youssef was asleep on a thin mattress on the kitchen floor. His lower body was covered by a sheet. It seemed as if he wasn't wearing any clothes. It was late summer and Um Adnan could see droplets of sweat on his hairless chest. Youssef couldn't have been much older than twenty and it was very rare to see an Arab man without hair on his chest. Um Adnan walked over to the fridge and poured herself a glass of water. She stood over Youssef and drank and drank. He was quite muscular from all the physical labor. His hair was a tousled dirty blond. Something quite common of men from Youssef's town. His skin was a golden shade of bronze. Apparently he had spent the earlier part of the summer working at his uncle's farm. Too much toiling around cow shit convinced him that it was time for bigger and better things. His move to Beirut was quick and drastic. And his subsequent affair with Um Adnan was something the whole neighborhood knew about, except for Abu Adnan.

"So you see Zena, these fights happen around once a month. Abu Adnan accuses his wife of having an affair, while Youssef sits and watches. On top of that, Abu Adnan has never complained that the renovations to his home are taking so long. Which makes us all guess that there is a suspicious relationship between Youssef and Abu Adnan too! It's a sordid mess. But we all pretend we don't know what's going on and just put up with the monthly fights for the entertainment value."

"Wow. I would have never guessed. I thought Youssef was their son."

"Well, he sure acts like it. That boy has been living under their roof for almost a year now. He sleeps, eats and screws for free. Welcome to your new neighborhood, Zena."

"And all this time, I thought Youssef was Adnan. Where the hell is Adnan?"

"Adnan is older. He is married and lives just down the street. Somehow everyone on this street is related in one way or another."

It was true. My own sister lives right above me.

And above them is Amira who is married to a nice German, Andreas. They have a kid and a very happy life. I hear Amira sometimes playing hide and seek with her kid in the stairwell. I wonder if I will ever be able to experience that pleasure. Listening to her is bittersweet. I want that life, but so often I have purposefully pushed it away. Listening to Amira, it seems so easy. It comes to her so naturally. It makes me smile.

I used to know her in university. I think her relationship with her best friend was a lot like Maya and mine. We all got married around the same time. Amira and her best friend got pregnant. Maya and I got divorces. A few weeks after Maya passed away I saw Amira at a bar. She told me she had just stopped breast-feeding and was so happy she could finally have a beer again. She was with her best friend. They were chatting about their kids. I ran out of the bar swearing that I never wanted to see her again. How could fate be so cruel? Why couldn't it have been Maya and me at that table? Why did I get left behind?

One year later, I moved into Amira's building. I wonder if it was fate playing her silly games with me. Or maybe this is just how Beirut is. Small.

Bittersweet.

Incestuous.

Inevitable.

Who knows ... maybe one day I will have children of my own

and maybe they will play with Amira's kids. Maybe they might even become childhood sweethearts and marry. It is possible.

Anything is possible here.

I am confident that I can find a man who can get me pregnant.

I want my Arab man on his horse, with his sword and poetry and wine.

23

In 1996, Kamal invited me to go and see a play with him.

I wasn't attracted to him, but I felt bad saying no. He was so nice and sweet.

There were only two semi-active theaters in Beirut at the time. After the war, it was difficult to get people to watch plays. I think the civil war proved to be a fifteen-year theatrical performance and Lebanese people were just plain saturated.

A few playwrights and actors determined not to let theater die in Lebanon, wrote a few plays a year, with what little funding they could get, just to keep the spirit of theater alive.

I cannot remember the name of the play we went to see. But I do remember what Kamal told me while we were buying our tickets.

I wore a long beige skirt. It had large blue and green blotches on it. I believe they meant to be abstract daises.

I think Kamal was trying to throw me a compliment when he said: "You look like a cow, but I love meat."

24

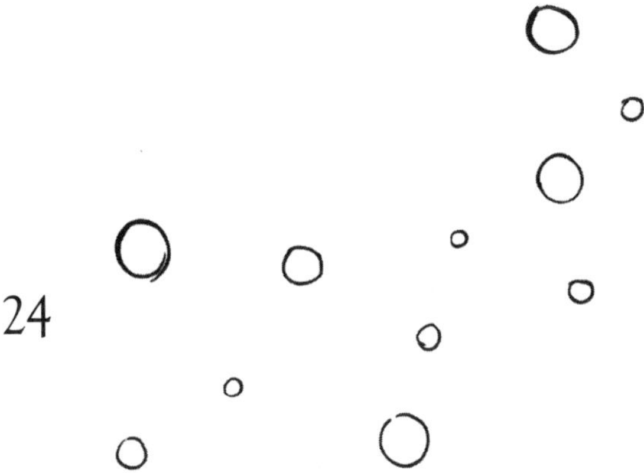

"Farah, how old are you?" I asked. I was shopping for some art supplies. Farah, a young girl, was assisting me. She pushed my cart around as I stocked up on glitter, beads and colored feathers.

"Miss Zena, I am fifteen years old."

"Are you still studying?"

"Yes, I am almost done with high school."

"What are you planning to do when you finish high school?"

"To be honest, I can't wait for the day I hear a man's lips call me his wife."

"Sure, that is a nice idea, but what do you want to do before that?"

"What else is there to do? God willing, I will hear those words very soon. It's nice to be married, isn't it? It must be the best thing in the world. I can't wait to take care of my husband. Feed him. Tickle him. Have his babies. And if the money isn't good, it doesn't matter because I know that God will send me the man that I need and deserve. Is that not so, Miss Zena?"

"Farah, you're asking the wrong woman. I just divorced my husband. I was tired of feeding him and washing his clothes. And also, he wasn't ticklish. And I think I just stopped believing in God."

"No, don't ever say that. God forgive her. God forgive you," she panicked, clasping her hands together and blowing a kiss to the ceiling.

"Farah, don't worry. God will forgive me, but she certainly won't forgive you if you don't finish your education. And blowing her kisses isn't going to get you on her good side. But having an education will."

"Miss Zena, I'm sorry, but I think I have to get back to work. I am sorry you are divorced, but maybe you got what you deserved."

"Thank you Farah, I'm sure I did."

I continued shopping, filled up my cart and pushed it to the check-out. The woman behind the desk looked down, avoiding my eyes and murmured that I should stack my things. Farah was standing behind her, fidgeting with her veil, also not making eye contact. I pulled out each item one by one. Slowly. Deliberately. I had pink satin ribbons. Purple shimmery plastic flowers. Gold glittery stars. Bags and bags of pink beads. All shapes. All sizes.

"Would you like to pay in dollars or Lebanese lira?"

"Dollars," I replied handing her my credit card. "Farah, this is what is going to make you happy – independence. After that, you can decide for yourself where and to whom you should put your energy into." I paid up and walked out of the store. I felt so bad. I fought her, while I should have embraced her. I guess I still contained some bitterness over my divorce. With a few words she was able to bring out a horrible person in me.

I dumped the stuff in my car, locked it up again, and called Nour, who lived down the street from the store.

"Nour! Hey, it's Zena. You'll never guess what just happened ... I was getting stuff for my installation and you know the young girl who works there ... Yeah, Farah ... Well I just got into a fight with her.

Can I come over for a bit?" Nour replied that I could, but warned me that she was in the middle of a waxing session. She thought a moment and then demanded that I come over immediately and get waxed too.

I walked down the street to Nour's house. She lived in an area of Beirut called *Mar Elias*. It's a religiously mixed neighborhood, which makes it slightly dangerous. Every time things get out of hand, politically, it always shows up first in *Mar Elias*. The Sunnis blame the Druze. The Druze threaten the Shiites. The Shiites point fingers at the Maronites. The Maronites vow to liberate Lebanon from the Muslims. A roadside bomb goes off. Tires are thrown into the middle of the street and set on fire.

Mar Elias in English means "Saint Elias".

Nour's apartment building was adorned with colorful string lights and ribbons. The entrance of the building was covered with palm leaves. All an indication that someone from her building had recently returned from Haj in Mecca.

I pushed my way through the leaves feeling a bit cynical.

I thought: and now they have to go and chop down trees, like we don't have enough environmental issues to deal with already.

I pressed the elevator call button; it lit up orange. Good, there was electricity. I was not going to walk up three flights of stairs in the heat. Stepping into the elevator, I whispered my usual elevator prayer, hoping for the electricity not to go off, hoping not to get stuck. Three floors up, I was met by her father at the door.

"Hi *Amo*, is Nour home?"

"Yes, yes, come in. She is busy in her room, please go ahead and excuse me for not following."

I walked down the corridor and knocked on her door.

"Who is it?"

"Who do you think?" I said, barging in.

Nour was sprawled on her bed and hovering over her was Awatief, the sugar wax woman. As I walked in, Awatief was ripping off some of her special gummy sugar wax from Nour's legs. Nour winced in pain, but gave me the thumbs up to come in and close the door.

"Hi Awatief, how are you? Giving Nour a hard time as usual?"

"You girls, I don't understand you. You leave your country and move to the West and start shaving. You start behaving like European woman. No time to eat. No time to fix your hair. No time to love. No time to wax. Look at this mess I have to deal with." Awatief started kneading a new ball of sugar wax and pressed it onto Nour's leg.

"Awatief, I just got a divorce. Please be nice to me."

"What? What did he do? Who is she? Tell me who she is and I will send my brothers after her!"

"Who says it was another woman? Why does it always have to be another woman? Why does it have to be his fault?"

"Who's fault could it be then ... yours? Are you in love with someone else? Ahhhh ... you little devil you. Who did you sleep with? And please don't tell me you started shaving too?"

"Awatief. I didn't sleep with anyone. And I really don't think he did either. I was just stagnant."

"Was he bad in the bedroom?"

"Honestly. I don't even know. I don't even know what is good or bad anymore. I have forgotten what love feels like. I have forgotten what it means to have tenderness. We were like wolves and there was never any pleasure. Not for him, or me."

"This is bad. You see. You see why I never married. Arab men, they are all crazy. They just want in and out. No kisses. No hugs. No tenderness."

"No Awatief, you can't judge like that. It has nothing to do with being Arab."

"Oh yes it does. We all sit here wondering when we are going to die, while the rest of the world goes about life in the most ordinary of ways. They are not always thinking about death the way we are. We are obsessed with death. We don't want to die, but we know that the sooner we die, the sooner we get to paradise. But then, it is only the men who get to paradise. So what becomes of us women? Nothing. We are here until the fucking forty virgins take over. So, who cares about tenderness? They don't care about that. They don't have to give anything, because they are going to get everything. They don't care about the now. So, their mentality is to fuck quickly today. And when and only when they reach paradise can they take their eternal time with their eternal virgins. The fucking eternal virgins who magically have their hymens reconstructed every night after severe fucking." With that she ripped the wax off Nour's other leg.

Nour shrieked in pain.

"Ya Awatief, you don't have to pull my skin off! I'm on your side. You left the sugar to stick for too long. Look, if you want to talk about men, wait until you're done waxing. Don't take it out on me. You think I haven't had my share? And besides it's not just Arab men who have problems. I was with a European for two years. They are not any better. At first he wined and dined me. And then he led me to believe that we were soul-mates and that the Earth was going to stop for us. I moved to Europe with him and naturally, started planning our lives together. I took charge, looked for a bigger apartment, and got a kick-ass job. Then one day, he just walked out. For no reason. He said that he didn't believe that I would leave my family in Beirut and move to Europe with him. I reminded the idiot that we were already in Europe and that I had already left Beirut. What the hell was his problem? He said that my family would never accept his. I asked him why that was relevant to our relationship. I was already living in sin with him in Europe and I was enjoying it very much and had no intentions of moving back to Beirut, let alone giving two shits what my family thought about him.

"He walked out that day. He just walked out and left me all alone in a strange city in a strange country. You know what? You know what it was? He couldn't stand to be with a real woman. He wanted a poor Arab woman that he could rescue. He wanted to be the colonial. The conqueror. He wanted to have me cry at his feet every night, thanking him for rescuing me from my poor and oppressive Muslim background. When he realized that we Arab women are neither poor, nor oppressed, he lost interest in me. That fucking bastard made me pack up my life and move to Europe and then he got bored. But I don't blame him. I blame myself for being so blind. The problem is not with men. It is with us. We are too smart for our own good. We should just play the game and be stupid. He wanted an oppressed Muslim, I should have been one. He wanted a woman who was submissive in bed. I should have been submissive. And clipped his fucking toenails with my teeth. Awatief, what's wrong with you. Stop looking at me like that. Come on, the sugar is getting cold. Get back to work."

"Nour, you know, it's not the end of the world. At least you got to see Europe. Not like me, stuck in the filthy city, having to wax women all day. Listening to their stupid gossip stories about who's sleeping around. And which government minister is on the payroll. And which political party is now accepting handouts from Amreeka. All while having to wax their old and haggard cunts, which they never use anyway. At least not with their husbands. And certainly not with lovers. God knows what they are sticking in their holes these days. Zena, by the way, since you're here, would you like a wax?"

"Why not?" I sat down on the chair opposite her. "Nour, did Awatief do your you know what?"

"Yes. You should do it too."

"No, no, I don't think so. If I do, it means I want to get laid or something. I just got divorced and really the last thing on my mind is to jump into bed with another guy."

"What about another woman?" Awatief snapped at me. "You think that only men should get the pleasure of licking a soft cunt?"

"Awatief! How can you talk like this? Please, I don't have a 'cunt', I have a 'punani'. Please respect it and call it by its name. And besides, I'm not going to be like all those women."

"Which ones?" Nour asked.

"You know, those women. Those Lebanese women who gave up on men ... and turned to women. I will not do that. I like men. I like to sleep with men. I'm just a bit fragile right now.'

Awatief started laughing and Nour followed. It started slow, but then grew louder until Awatief started laughing with tears. "Please, please stop. I can't laugh anymore, I am going to piss my pants."

"What? What did I say?"

"You are so funny ... Come here. Sit here. I will wax your little puna ... punan ... what did you call it? I will wax it for free today. And you will see. In three weeks, when your little hairs start to grow back, you will call me and ask for another wax. Why? Because you will have had the best sexual experience of your life. Whether you choose to do it with a man or a woman is up to you. But whatever the case, please do it soon because I swear to God, if you ever tell me that you are 'fragile' again, I will send God's mercenaries after you. But unlike those fucking virgins, you will never heal. Zena, you cannot be fragile and live in Beirut. You cannot. It doesn't mix. If you want to be fragile, go to Amreeka. They have those talk shows there and you can talk all about your feelings and about how fragile you are. They love that stuff there. Here if you tell someone you are fragile, you are inviting them to willingly fuck with your head. Now, come sit down and I will make you a real woman. Take off your pants and spread your legs. I will not hurt you."

It hurt like hell.

With every yank of the sugar mix, I saw stars. She started on the top and worked her way down between my legs. When she reached my most sensitive area, I almost fainted from the pain. "Please. Please stop. I can't take it anymore."

"I can't stop now. It is unfinished and I never leave anything unfinished. One more time. Hold on."

I lay on the bed with my legs apart, looking like I was about to give birth. She spread the sugar just over my clitoris and pulled. I screamed and Nour put her hand over my mouth, because after all, we were in her bedroom and her parents were just down the hall. They of course knew that we were being waxed, but there was no need to shout out that we had decided to do our private parts too. At that moment my cell phone rang. It was my sister.

"Hello? Hello? Zena, are you OK?" Her voice sounded panicked.

"No, not really. If only you knew what just happened."

"I know, I know! Are you OK? Were you next to it? Mom is OK, by the way."

"Lana, what do you mean? What's wrong with mom?!"

"Zena, there was a bomb. Just outside Mom's office. It just went off like two minutes ago. She's OK though ... where are you?"

I was stunned. I started crying.

"I am OK, Lana. I am OK. I am at Nour's. Don't worry. Listen, I'll call you back later. Call everyone and make sure we're all accounted for. I can't talk." I hung up and tried calling my mom. It wasn't connecting. "Shit! It's not connecting!"

"Zena, what's wrong? Another bomb? Where was it? Is everyone OK?" Nour was filling a glass of water for me. "Here, drink this and calm down."

"I'm fine. I'm fine. Awatief, please finish. We can't call anyone anyways. The lines are all jammed now. Everyone is trying to call everyone. Awatief, please finish this. I want to have some dignity when I walk out of here today. Don't leave me looking half finished." I thought about the photograph Man Ray took of himself, when he shaved only half of his face. It's funny the things that cross your mind in times of stress.

The rest of the waxing continued in silence. It was over in a few minutes. I went to the bathroom, washed and got dressed. Awatief had already left by then. I sat next to Nour in silence.

"Zena, do you realize that at the same moment you screamed the bomb went off."

"Yes, that is all I have been thinking about. At the same moment Awatief was glorifying my sexual organs, someone lost their father, brother, sister, mother, friend. I almost lost my mom. Imagine my mom was leaving her office early today, or crossing the street to get a bite to eat, or picking up a package ... she could have been ... gone. Gone with the bomb.

And when people ask me what I was doing when the bomb went off, I would have to tell them I was getting my cunt waxed.

"It's too much. Nour, it's too much. I have to get out of here. We have to leave. I can't do anything normally anymore."

"Leave. Where will we go? You think I can get a visa just like that?"

I looked down at my feet, feeling a little guilty because deep down inside I knew how lucky I was to have a foreign passport. I could leave anytime. I could go anywhere. Nour, Nour could be stuck here forever. "Don't worry, I won't leave you," I said to her. "I didn't leave Maya and I won't leave you."

"Thank God Maya didn't stick around for this mess. She got out at the right time. She is free now. Not like us."

"Nour, come here. Don't worry. Everything is going to be OK. I can feel it. We are going to be OK. We don't need anything to convince us except for ourselves. Come on and get dressed. Let's go get a drink at Torino. I'm sure everyone is going to be there tonight. We have to console each other. And besides we have punanis as smooth as a baby's butt. Let's go have a drink."

"Zena, I thought you weren't ready to meet people."

"I'm not. But when bombs go off, you realize that life is too short to be fragile. Let's go make Awatief proud. Men ... women ... I'll take what I can get tonight."

"Wow, Zee! I like this new you."

"We dodge bombs. This is our reality. We have to live it. We cannot deny where we live. Otherwise, spare yourself the agony and move to Europe and ride the subway in peace."

"The subway? Don't you know they're blowing up the subways now too?"

"OK, so there you have it. Wherever you are in the world, you are eventually going to die. So, do you risk the bomb on the European subway or do you take your chances with Beirut. Me, I would choose Beirut any day. At least if I die here I will get a proper funeral. In Europe, if I die. I will die alone. And if I happened to forget my wallet at home that day, as I usually do, people may never even know who I am. Who my body is. Can you say that? Is that grammatically correct? Who my body is?"

I tried calling my mom again and still no connection.

"Zena, do you think one day we can talk about these days in the past? Do you think we will be able to say things like 'Hey, remember those days the bombs went off like every other day ... jeez, that was so long ago ... it almost seems like it was all a dream.'"

"Honestly, no."

"Yeah. I don't think so either. At least not in this lifetime."

"And definitely not with the kind of neighbors we have. As long as their issue is unresolved, we will have to live with bombs."

"I agree. I think we should send Awatief over the border and have her wax the crap out of everyone. And then we should pass along a big fat joint and have all our politicians smoke up. Then they can all go and fuck themselves because I'm sick and tired of them fucking me."

I burst out laughing. "Nour, if we don't leave now for that drink, no one will be kissing you tonight."

I tried calling mom again.

Still couldn't get through.

25

If it isn't bombs, it's roadblocks.

If it isn't our neighbors, it's internal.

Beirut. Violence. Love. Family. Life.

This is life.

I had to leave Beirut for a few weeks. It was the first time I had traveled alone in years. I was invited to go to Oslo for a conference. My first official conference. It felt good. I was feeling strong and independent again. I wanted to take a positive side of Beirut and share it with the rest of the world. Things were going well. The conference was a success. I spoke of Beirut. And though I had only been gone a few days, there was nostalgia in my voice, a sweet tone that surprised people.

While in Beirut, running away seems to be the number one priority on our list. As soon as we set one foot outside, we are miserable. We miss her. We realize how beautiful she is. We only see the good things. The love. The family. The mountains. The sea. The good and fresh food. The coffee that tastes like coffee. The jokes that make you laugh for hours. Your grandmother's wrinkles. The history. The culture. The warmth.

The security.

At the conference, I tried to explain that in Lebanon we enjoyed a sense of freedom that is incomparable to the rest of the world. That out of all the countries in the Middle East, Lebanon most highly valued freedom of speech and expression.

But then Hind called me from Beirut.

She said that overnight, Hezbollah and Amal militias blockaded the streets with the intention of bringing the city to a halt. Apparently it was some sort of a people's strike. It had been going on for a few days. She could not believe it. It was as if we hadn't gone through enough shit already in the past two years.

She decided to go to the beach. This was her form of resistance. It had been two days since she had been allowed to go to work and she could not take staying at home any longer. All major roads that led to her neighborhood were blocked, but she was determined to find a way out. It was the beginning of summer and she was not going to let them ruin it. She took a back street from her home and drove towards the bridge leading to downtown Beirut. Knowing that there would most probably be checkpoints on top of the bridge, she decided to take the tunnel below. It was a long tunnel. The one where they dumped bodies during the civil war. Like most of us, driving through that tunnel always sent shivers down her spine. But this was the quickest way to get to her destination and she pressed down hard on the accelerator. She was determined to get through the tunnel as quickly as possible. It was pitch black. The electricity had been cut off. She turned on her high beams. She was the only one in the tunnel. Most people, in fear of the demonstrations and blockades, had decided to stay at home. Trying not to think about anything, Hind pushed on. Slowly she began to see the tiny light at the end of the tunnel. Almost there, she thought to herself. This wasn't so bad after all.

But Beirut is full of surprises. And just as Hind reached the end of the tunnel a young man stepped out of the shadows and onto the middle of the street. She slammed the breaks and brought her car to a halt. Her pulse was jacked up and she suddenly had a bitter taste in her mouth. He was dressed in civilian clothing, but was carrying a weapon all too familiar with her. The Kalashnikov. She told me that she recognized it because she had seen it in my artwork so many times. The wooden handle and curved rectangular cartridge box were unmistakable. She remembered the stories from the civil war. The ones about how you could be killed at a checkpoint if your religion was in question. But these were different times. There was no civil war.

She told herself to stay in control.

She lowered her window and smiled politely, "Sorry, I didn't see you."

"It's OK. I was hiding on purpose." He couldn't have been more than seventeen years old. Looking over his face, Hind noticed his mustache was still soft. He had never shaved it before.

"Can I pass?" Hind asked politely, but firmly.

"Sorry, but you cannot go through. All roads are blocked. Where did you come from?"

Hind, not sure whether she should tell him or not, looked away.

"It's OK. I will not kill you. There is no civil war. Just tell me where you came from so I can tell you how to get back."

"*M'saitbeh*," she looked straight into his eyes. How could she be afraid of someone half her age?

"OK, I am sorry to tell you that you are going to have to reverse the same way you came in. You cannot turn, there is not enough space for the car to turn. You have to reverse."

"What?" Hind looked at him in disbelief. "That's impossible. Do you know how long this tunnel is?"

"I'm sorry. It's for your protection. I'm Sunni like you. I'm trying to protect you from the Shiite who have set up a checkpoint just down the street. You should be lucky I was here to protect you."

"I thought I shouldn't have to worry as we are not having a civil war. Now you are telling me that had I crossed through, the Shiites would have killed me? Make up your mind. Anyways, are we not all Muslims? When did this rupture happen?"

"They cannot be trusted. That is all I am saying. Now, please start reversing." His grip tightened on his gun and Hind, not wanting any more trouble, rolled up her window and put her car into reverse. She had to stop several times along the way to redirect her focus. Moving backwards can be a bit disorienting. Until finally, she was out. Still determined to go to the beach, she took a side street away from the tunnel. She drove through a neighborhood she had never seen before in her life. There were banners of Hezbollah and Amal martyrs. Great, she thought, straight into another lion's den. The streets were empty though, so she decided it might be best to simply park the car and then continue by foot. She already had a view of the sea so how long could it possibly take?

She parked next to an overfilled dumpster and made sure to take off her windshield wipers before locking the car. The previous ones had been stolen only a few weeks earlier when she had parked in a similar neighborhood. What is funny is that we have now begun to stereotype neighborhoods based on religious confessions. What Hind didn't know was that the neighborhood in which her wipers were stolen was in fact, Sunni. Her people stole from her.

Theft is not racist.

She picked up her beach bag and threw on a cardigan for good measure. One could not be too sure about exposing their shoulders in a neighborhood like this.

Fast forward to our phone call. It took her an hour and a half to get to the beach, but she made it. And she was prepared to keep doing this until a consensus had been reached.

"Zena, you don't understand. It's not about the beach. It's about being able to get from one side of my city to the other. No one owns it. Especially not a seventeen-year-old with a fucking gun. Those days are over. There is no civil war. They called for civil disobedience and I gave it to them. They can all go and fuck themselves for all I care. All of them. The government and the so-called opposition."

"Hiiiined," I pronounced her name with a heavy Lebanese accent, "I miss Beirut. Why do I feel nostalgic? I feel like I should have been on that journey with you. But here I am in Oslo, so far away." I had been staring down at the pavement during the whole conversation, but now I looked up. I was sitting in Oslo's new development by the sea, Aker Brygge. To my left, fishermen were returning from their day at work. People were lining up to buy fresh shrimp straight off the boats. In front of me was the newly established Nobel Peace Center. On my right, the large brown façade of the City Hall. It was in this hall that the Nobel recipients were awarded their medal every year in December. It was a stark contrast to the conversation I was having with Hind.

"I want to come home," I said. How was it that in this beautiful place, tranquil and serene, all I could think about was being thrown into an insecure and violent place? When I could have calm waters and rolling green hills, I wanted stress and concrete. But was it really that? Beirut had to be more than that. It is a lot more than that.

I would rather have a bit of instability, knowing that it makes me a stronger person. I would rather sit on my balcony any day and watch my crazy neighbors; father and son, walk around in their boxers because it sweltering hot and there is no electricity for the air conditioner. I would rather have a morning coffee with Um Tarek and her fabulous stories than sit here on this peaceful jetty, all alone. I would rather stay up all night reading poetry with friends, about Beirut, war, love, drugs, death, and irony. I would rather pray in the morning and thank God for granting me one more day than lay my head down at night taking for granted that I will wake up the next day. I would rather walk on dusty streets listening to DAM on my I-pod and dream up ways to liberate my Palestinian friends. I would rather walk on the Corniche with my friend, the poet, stay up all night talking about politics, and then deliriously fall into his arms as the sun creeps up behind *our* mountains. I would rather drink tea with my aunt Nabila in Aley. I would rather visit Iyad's family in Baalbeck, they always insist on stuffing my car with labneh, bread and all sorts of fresh vegetables when I'm leaving. I would rather have lunch by a river in the Shouf and eat watermelon and feta cheese with my cousins. I would rather visit Nayiri and have her read my coffee grounds. I would rather be close to Maya's grave.

I would rather water my garden and tend to my gardenia plant as she is an old friend. I would rather take Sara out for sushi on Abed al Wahab Street. I would rather lose myself momentarily for one night of decadence with nightlife royalty, my beloved Clefies and Babycakes, I would rather take Tapi out for a walk, wearing my smelly sandals, savoring every step in Beirut. I would rather listen to Murjan play his guitar on my rooftop. I would rather go dancing with Susan and watch as her hips sway so naturally to spirited live Arabic music. I would rather have breakfast with Lena by the sea. I would rather have brunch with Christine and Bawsee. I would rather listen to Hind read her poetry at Zico House. I would rather eat a french fry sandwich on Hamra Street. I would rather make love in my purple bedroom with high ceilings and the mosque ringing in my ears. I would rather paint in the studio with Halleh. I would rather stop for a coffee at Café Younis and accidently run into Dahna on the street. I would rather buy chocolate and water from Abu Talal. I would rather ride my bicycle with Ramzi. I would rather drink Mojitos with Marya, his mother, at Pacifico with the lovely waiter who loves Tapi.

I would rather walk the streets of Beirut, retracing steps I once took with Mazen. With Makram. With Maya.

I would rather be close to my family. I would rather have Lana above my head, Nemo down the street and Seif in my heart.

I would rather sit on Amira and Andreas's hammock on our roof and listen to them play with their son. I would rather watch Ginou fire dance in a Cedar forest. I would rather watch Simba's dreadlocks sway in the wind by a beach in Beirut. In Beirut. In Beirut.

"Habibti," her voice softened, "even if I were to let you, you can't come. The airport has been shut down. We have no idea how long this will go on."

Our airport was shut down two summers ago.

It has been shut down again.

History repeats itself.

"Hind, I love you. Take care of yourself and have a beer for me. Everyone here is so polite. No one drinks on the streets. I want a beer, but am too shy to walk into a pub alone. Have one for me."

"Already there, my dear, already there. I'm having it Mexican, with lemon and salt."

"Don't tell me these things. I'm very lonely here all by myself."

The line cut.

A few days later, I was in London. Trying to get home. One step closer. I felt like I could finally release. A little. I spent the whole day on the phone talking to everyone I loved. Knowing that my phone bill was going to skyrocket, I called anyway. What is the price you are willing to pay to speak to someone who could be dead the next day?

After the calls I went down to the streets to walk, hoping to run into someone who could comfort me. But who? I am alone in this city.

I bought a newspaper in Arabic even though I couldn't read it. I bought it to carry around. Maybe if someone saw the Arabic, they would stop me and ask if I had heard the news about Lebanon. The newspaper in my hand would be a flag. I wanted to connect to another Arab. I thought that if he saw the newspaper, he would stop me and ask. Then I would say yes, I had heard the news. And how was it that he knew I was Lebanese. To which he would reply: "Oh my dear, you are holding a newspaper in Arabic. And more so, it's the way you are holding it. Clutched close to your heart. You must be Lebanese. Have you only just found out? Are you all right? Is your family OK?"

Knowing that my little trick had worked I would reply, "You know, I am so glad you stopped me. I was on the verge of tears. I just had to talk to someone about the situation. I am Zena, by the way."

"I am Karim. I'm also from Lebanon. Would you like to join me for some tea?"

To which I would reply, "Karim, I never talk to strangers, but it's funny how war can make you break all the rules. Let's have some tea."

We would then walk a block and sit down at the first caféwe find.

"Karim, I feel so alienated. The media here is not talking about the situation back home. Why is that?"

"Well, I guess you haven't read your article yet. It said in the papers today that Hezbollah rallied against pro-Western media outlets. They have locked down some major TV stations and newspapers. They are not allowing the foreign press to take pictures either."

I would look down at the newspaper and looking back up, notice that Karim has disappeared. Where did he go? Without even saying goodbye.

The newspaper is still clutched close to my heart.

I am alone.

My relationship with Hezbollah has always been a strange one. When I first moved to Beirut I was afraid of them. Growing up outside Lebanon, we were taught by Western media that Hezbollah is a terrorist organization. A force so evil, their only intent was total world domination. I was so afraid of them I never dared to even utter their name. They say that if you think of something or say it, you will it to come to you. I imagined them to be a gang of dark-bearded men enshrouded by an evil green fog. One encounter with them would leave you dead as a doornail. I believed all that until the day I actually met one of "them".

I was in Dahiyeh, the southern suburb of Beirut, taking pictures without a permit. It was for a university project and I had no idea how tight security was and that I actually did need a permit to take photographs in that part of town. The theme of my project was Lebanese women. I wanted to portray the abounding variety of religious and social strata in our country. I wanted to document how open we were, wanted to show how a woman wearing a chador from head to toe could be seen walking next to a blond in a miniskirt.

You know. The usual thing people say when they are trying to speak highly of Lebanese women and the openness of our society. Without realizing it, I found myself very close to Hezbollah headquarters. I hadn't paid attention to how far I'd wandered into Dahiyeh – I was mesmerized by beautiful pools of colored veils of multiple sizes and textures. The sun was high, casting shadows on the eyes exposed by the veils.

With my concentration placed solely on my viewfinder, I failed to notice a short, stocky man hobbling towards me. He confronted me and my camera and asked me to follow him, saying that I needed a special permit to take photos in that area. He took me to a building and then they escorted me to another and before I knew it, I was inside a Hezbollah interrogation center.

I was treated kindly and with respect. They called me sister. They politely asked me to take off my shoes before I went in. My Doc Martins stuck to my skin because of the summer heat, but I did manage to take them off. I hoped that my feet did not smell. I was taken into a room about one and a half meters by three. There was a mirror. Like the ones in the movies, where you know that someone behind is watching you. On the other side there was a huge flag that draped the wall. It was pink and had green calligraphy on it. I wished I read Arabic so that I could know what it said.

But it was baby-pink and that is something I will never forget.

They asked me a few questions. Why was I in this part of town? Why was I taking pictures? I answered all their questions and after twenty minutes, they released me. Nadim and Maya were with me that day. We were all put into separate rooms and we all answered their questions the same way. We were released, but my film was left with them.

"Please understand Sister Zena, we have to take precautions. This is for your safety. And for the protection of our great country."

They called me a week later and told me I could come and pick up my film. It was safe. I hadn't taken any pictures they considered to be a breach of security. It was funny – I had not left my phone number with them. They developed and printed my pictures for free.

After this experience, I realized that nothing is as it seems in the world. It was important to question everything. And I'm still trying to figure things out. It may take a long time. It may take my entire life.

Arabs in Hollywood movies are always portrayed the same way. But is this who we really are? Having a Western-backed government and promoting democracy sounds good on paper, but Western-backed institutions also include the Abu Ghraib prison, Guantanamo, the invasions of Iraq, Afghanistan and Vietnam, McDonalds and Bush's not-so-White House.

It includes a summer war.

Beirut, cut me some slack. Does it always have to be this complicated?

26

I have a fever.

I am not sure how long I have been like this. And no one knows for sure what caused it.

My mother sits beside my bed. She has not slept in days. She is reading a book about our religion. She is trying to find God so that she may ask him to let me live. In our religion there are very few books that still exist, and she was lucky to find one in English. It is 1982, and there is only one such book currently available. She had it shipped to us in Africa. She wanted it in English so she could read it out loud to me. She wanted to make sure that I understood every single word.

It is the very first time I've had malaria. It is the very first time I hear fear in my mother's voice. I cannot lift my arms. I cannot swallow. I can hardly find the strength to breathe. It is hot, but there are three fans on me. I feel like I am slipping, but not sure where I am going.

My mother continues to read. This goes on for days. Maybe weeks. I lose track of time. Days become nights and nights are endless.

I would go on to contract malaria at least four more times during my childhood.

About ten years ago, I went to the Red Cross office in Beirut to donate blood. They refused. They said my blood was unclean because I had had malaria so many times. About five years ago, my mother was in a terrible accident. I went to the hospital to give her some of my blood. They refused. They said it was not clean enough. My mother got her blood from complete strangers that day.

Thank you, I guess.

I have a fever.

I am not sure how long I have been like this for. And no one knows for sure how it is that I came to be like this.

I am eight years old. A few days ago I was playing outside on the streets. Dia got hungry. I invited him over for lunch, but he said he was too shy to come into our big house. He said we could walk down to the end of the street and buy some suya from a vendor. I told him he'd have to go alone, as I was not allowed to go far from the house. He looked at me very perplexed and almost hurt.

"Eeeets OK fo me to come to yo big white house, but not OK fo you to walk wit me to buy black man food?"

I was embarrassed. He had a point.

"Dia, sorry. You are right. Come, I go wit you."

We walked away from the big iron gates that protected our home. Protected is the word my family used. Barricaded is the word I prefer. It was a hot day in February. There was not a single cloud in the sky. Dia took my hand.

"Don't worry. No body go touch you."

I squeezed back, took a deep breath and walked with him.

As we walked, sand from the dusty road slid into my sandals. I didn't want to stop and clean them out. I was afraid of drawing too much attention. Nigerians never stopped to clean out their sandals. The earth was part of their body and spirit. I wanted to be like that too.

Halfway down the street, I could already smell the suya. The vendor had just put a few slices of meat on the barbeque and was using a folded newspaper as a fan to get the coals burning. It smelled good.

"*Ekaro*!" Dia greeted the vendor in Yoruba. "suya please." The vendor looked up at me and asked Dia if it was for one person only. "No," he replied, "suya fo two wit plenty pepe."

The vendor shrugged and handed Dia two steamy slices. Dia wrapped one in a newspaper and handed it to me. As I unfolded it I was surprised to see that the meat was orange.

"Dia, dis meat be orange. I no get sick?"

"No, de orange ees pepe. If you want be like us Nigerians you haf to learn to eet pepe."

I ate the suya. It was hotter than anything I could have ever imagined. Tears rolled down my face. But it didn't stop me. I ate the whole thing. Dia and the vendor began to laugh at my tears. The vendor sang to me:

Oyebo pepe
If you eate pepe
You go yello
More more!
White man,
If you eat pepper
You will turn red,
More and more.

Dia took my hand and led me back home. He was as proud of me as I was. I was a crying Nigerian.

From that day on, I would continue to buy suya.

And cry.

I have a fever.

I jump on top of the couch and start singing from the top of my lungs. I am hallucinating. It is an incredible rush. I am sick, but I don't feel sick. I have beat death so many times. This is really starting to become a piece of cake.

This fever.

I shoot a bird and it falls right out of the sky. It's the first time I've deliberately killed a bird. At first I am so happy. Happy because I actually made the shot. I am thirteen years old and trigger happy. The bird falls from the sky and I run to it.

Her wings are still moving. Her entire body shakes violently. She's dying. It hadn't been a clear shot.

I spin around and vomit. I am disgusted with myself.

The bird's eye looks straight at me. She knows what I've done and will not forgive me. I faint and fall to the ground. A few days later I am in bed with a fever. I dream about the bird. She has been haunting me. The more I try and push her away, the worse the fever gets.

But this time, I am not helpless in bed. Her bird spirit has taken over my body and I am running around the house flapping my arms.

I am standing on the couch singing.

I am singing like a bird.

I have a fever.

This time I want it to last.

His body is grinding up against mine. He is driving me crazy. My body responds to his.

I am thirty-two years old. We are at a rave. We dance under the green laser lights. I put one hand on his hip and the other on his back. The music is getting louder. He pulls me in closer to him. Our hips are joined. We dance around in circles. We are making love with our clothes on.

In the middle of the dance floor.

To the sound of large drums.

Surrounded by five thousand people. We are making love.

In Beirut.

I am delirious.

I bring my hand up to his head and pull at his hair. We are so close that I can smell his breath. It is sweet. It is good.

I whisper into his ear, "I love Beirut."

We start to kiss.

It is good.

I am so far away from death.

Acknowledgments

I would like to thank, first and foremost, Samar Hammam, who found me during the 2006 invasion of Lebanon. Through her wise and gentle nature, and her fiery passion and firm beliefs, Samar convinced me that this book had to be written. She has been my constant guide, the light that led the way. Samar, I am forever indebted to you.

Maya, though our time together was cut short, I am grateful for every second of our friendship. I have no doubt that we'll meet again – see you next time around. I'll be looking out for your halo.

I would also like to thank my wonderful family for their love, compassion, and generosity and for never leaving my side, even through the most difficult times. I would especially like to thank May and Faysal (mom and dad), Lana, Nidal, Diana, Sari, Karma, Naji, Kimo, Rakan, Anmar, Suha and my aunt Nabila.

To everyone at Saqi Books, thank you so much. I am deeply grateful for your commitment to *Beirut, I Love You*. Special thanks to Shikha Sethi, Lara Frankena, Anna Wilson, and Salwa Gaspard.

A special thank you to Toby Eady Associates; Toby, Samar, Jamie, Laetitia and everyone else at the office.

Last but not least, thank you Beirut for the chain of events you threw my way. Everything happens for a reason.

To my dear friends in and around Beirut, thank you for your love, support and guidance. Special thanks to Hiba Mikdashi, Sara and the Ghannoums, Marya and Ramzi Hibri, Christine O'Heron, Hind Shoufani, Mira Ghannoum, Imad Khachan, Susan, Lena, Saseen, Chafic, Mary Jo, Karen, Morgie, Zeus, Camille, Nayiri, Raytch, Alberto, Dana, Karima, Renito and Tapi.

To anyone else I may have forgotten to mention, please forgive me. You are in my heart.